7 Steps

To A

Better Portfolio

EDWARD JAMES GOODFELLOW

One Printers Way
Altona, MB R0G 0B0
Canada

www.friesenpress.com

Copyright © 2023 by Edward James Goodfellow
First Edition — 2023

All rights reserved.

No part of this publication may be reproduced in any form, or by any means, electronic or mechanical, including photocopying, recording, or any information browsing, storage, or retrieval system, without permission in writing from FriesenPress.

ISBN
978-1-03-916664-6 (Hardcover)
978-1-03-916663-9 (Paperback)
978-1-03-916665-3 (eBook)

1. BUSINESS & ECONOMICS, PERSONAL FINANCE, INVESTING

Distributed to the trade by The Ingram Book Company

Important Note

The book contains the opinion and views of the author and not necessarily those of his employers. The book does not represent a recommendation of any particular security, strategy, or investment product. The opinions of the author are subject to change without notice.

All efforts have been made to assure the accuracy and integrity of the information presented in the book. Although all the facts have been obtained from sources believed to be reliable, the information is not guaranteed and neither the author nor publisher is liable for any errors, omissions, or contradictions found in the text.

Investment and investing strategies should be evaluated based on one's own objectives. Readers should use their best judgment and consult a financial expert prior to making an investment decision based on the information found in this book.

Dedication

To Annastasia, Sabrina, Natasha, Gabriela, and Felicity for all their love and support.

About the Author

Edward Goodfellow is an associate portfolio manager in the Victoria, British Columbia (BC), office of PI Financial Corp., an associate faculty at Royal Roads University, and a sessional lecturer for the CPA Western School of Business. Edward is a Chartered Professional Accountant (CPA/CA), a Chartered Financial Analyst (CFA), a Certified Financial Planner (CFP), and a member of the Victoria Estate Planning Council.

A lifelong learner, Edward credits his undergraduate instructors at the University of Lethbridge for starting his journey into finance and accounting and his search into understanding the math and psychology of investing.

Edward lives on his farm in Metchosin in Victoria, BC, Canada.

Investing is a series of decisions around risk, return, time, and odds.

Why are you investing?
Where do returns come from?
What is risk?
How does one capture return and manage risk?

Portfolio investing is math and emotion.
Math is how you should build and structure a portfolio.
Emotion is why you don't.

Three Investment Objectives:

1) Capture returns in the ever-evolving capital markets
2) Manage risks in the ever-changing investment landscape
3) Increase the odds of accomplishing objective #1 and #2

Whether you are investing $100,000, $1,000,000, $10,000,000 or $100,000,000 your investment objective is to give yourself the best odds of capturing return and managing risk to meet your current and future cash flow needs.

Table of Contents

Introduction: 7 Steps to a Better Portfolio xiii

Chapter 1: Investment Dilemma 1

Chapter 2: Investment Journey 12

Chapter 3: Risk and Return 24

Chapter 4: Predictions and Expectations 40

Chapter 5: Strategy and Execution 49

Chapter 6: Markets 60

Chapter 7: Capturing Return and Managing Risk 71

Chapter 8: Three Portfolio Approaches 86

Chapter 9: 7 Steps to a Better Portfolio 93

    Step 1: Allocate across global capital markets 94

    Step 2: Diversify broadly within markets 98

    Step 3: Focus on higher expected returns 99

    Step 4: Utilize financial science 100

    Step 5: Manage strategy risk 103

    Step 6: Manage investment choice risk 105

    Step 7: Manage cost and taxes 107

Chapter 10: Evaluation Rubric 110

Chapter 11: Sample Portfolio 122

Chapter 12: Keep it Simple / Keep it Intelligent 128

Appendix 1: The Stock Picking Game 136

Appendix 2: Size Premium 150

Appendix 3: Value Premium 153

Appendix 4: Profitability Premium 157

Appendix 5: Randomness of Asset Class Returns 160

Introduction

7 Steps to a Better Portfolio

Millions of investors are just like you. They work most of their adult lives to earn an income. They forgo consuming some of that income to save for retirement. They invest and put at risk their savings to attain a return, as a means to grow their wealth. This wealth will provide for their consumption during retirement and fulfill any wishes they may have for their estate.

Investors seek a return. It's that simple! It's that complicated! Risk, the origin of return, is seldom understood by investors. Risk is something that hits you in the gut; it's palpable uncertainty. It makes you worry something is going on, but you are unaware or uninformed of what is happening. Return and risk should be at the core of all investment and portfolio decisions. The better you and your advisors understand how markets work, the risks of investing, and how you react to risks, the better equipped you are to make informed investment decisions.

Investing is complicated and full of uncertainty and noise. Markets, an investment fund, or a specific stock, may rise or fall at any given time, creating euphoria, fear, panic, or indifference. Meanwhile the media, social media, and social circles contribute to shifting feelings of uncertainty and optimism.

It does not matter how anyone else manages their investments. What matters is what you do. What you need to do is utilize a rules-based systematic investment process and structure. This approach will provide clarity, reduce the impact of investment noise, and facilitate better decision-making analysis. This approach will keep you focused on the goal of capturing returns and managing risks. The approach will provide more consistency and reliability of estimated returns data to enhance long-term financial planning. A rules-based, systematic investment process and structure improves your odds of long-term investment success.

Long-term success is about understanding the odds and managing the risk of being wrong. As an investor, it is important that you understand the difference between the compensating risks and returns and the non-compensating risks and returns. In simple terms, investing is about accepting the risks that are compensated with returns and avoiding ill-conceived risky bets. Other than the thrill, these risks are unlikely to result in the desired outcome.

Successful long-term investing, like a long and rewarding life, will be determined by the quality of your decisions and the framework used to evaluate those decisions. The quality of your decisions will largely depend on what information is evidence based and what is opinion based. Years and decades of good investing habits, focused on the variables you can control, can better help you address the variables you cannot control. The formation of good investing habits, resulting from quality decisions, can lead to a more enjoyable investment experience.

I wrote *7 Steps to a Better Portfolio* for you, the average long-term investor, to help identify, evaluate, and deal with critical investment issues. Whether you invest independently or alongside your advisor, *7 Steps* is an investment framework to help facilitate better decision-making along your investment journey, reduce investment stress, and improve your odds of long-term investment success.

I hope you enjoy the book.

Contact the author:

www.7stepstoabetterportfolio.com

www.edwardgoodfellow.ca

Chapter 1

Investment Dilemma

Something is happening!

Markets, interest rates, pandemics, inflation, geopolitics, stocks, Donald Trump, and so on, and so on. There is never-ending news that could affect your emotions, your views about investing, and the value of your investments. There are endless investment opinions and ideas telling you what is happening and what to do next. Markets, like many things, always seem to be in flux. You are challenged to make sense of the ever-changing financial world. You are worried something is happening, but you're not sure what it is, what it means, or what you should do.

What's the deal with investing?

Markets are an ever-evolving, asset-pricing mechanism affected by participants' views of new information. The repricing that results can be volatile, resulting in increased wealth or wealth destruction.

What's the deal with investing? You can't put your finger on it.

You should reframe the question to . . .

What's my strategy?

Rather than focus on short-term investing, think long-term. Rather than worry about what you do not control, focus on what you can control. Rather than indecision, think rules based. Rather than be reactive, be proactive. Rather than intuitive investing, think evidence based. Rather than be influenced by noise, think accuracy and clarity. Rather than worry about what is happening to others, think: what is my strategy?

START DEVELOPING A BETTER STRATEGY TODAY

We are all looking for an answer. Lose weight, be happier, get a promotion at work, become a better parent, get the most out of life. We are all seeking a solution or direction for making something better. Investing is no different. To some, investing solutions may be about timing markets, picking stocks, or finding the next Apple or the next Warren Buffet. *7 Steps* takes a different approach; it focuses on creating a portfolio process and structure to improve the odds of long-term investment success.

Put your question on a white board and think about it

Rather than trying to beat the odds with random bits of information, *7 Steps* focuses on the math of how markets work to put the odds in your favor. *7 Steps* examines important investment variables that investors control to better manage the variables they do not control. *7 Steps* is an investment decision-making framework to help investors be more accountable, build emotional resilience, encourage forward thinking, and instill confidence as they journey into the uncertain world of investing. Start developing a better strategy today; you will be grateful tomorrow.

Intention and Attention - We often have good intentions, like improve our health and investing returns. However we underestimate the required attention and steps it requires to achieve the desired result.

INVESTORS SEEK A RETURN.
IT'S THAT SIMPLE! IT'S THAT COMPLICATED!

The investor's motivation to invest is the expectation of achieving a financial return and the emotional reward of being correct.

A return is simple:

- A return is a win.
- A return is validation that you are correct.
- A return makes you feel smart.
- A return makes you feel safe.
- A return is a growth of wealth.
- A return is an emotional boost.
- A return is a bet that you won.

A return is what you are looking for! A return is affirmation that you made the right decision. Seeking a return is easy. You just buy something and hope it goes up. When it goes up, a gain or return on your investment can seem like money falling from the sky. How complicated can that be? The source of that return and understanding the risks and possible losses associated with attaining that return can be complicated.

Losses are what you don't want to happen! Losses are events you didn't expect. The worse the loss, the more it may affect your feelings and finances.

Losses can be complicated:

- A loss is confirmation that you are wrong.
- A loss is uncomfortable.
- A loss is reduction in your wealth and may cause financial hardship.
- A loss can be an emotional drain.
- A loss is a bet you lost.
- A loss feels like a punch to the gut.
- A loss is palpable uncertainty.
- A loss is frustrating.
- A loss can make you worry that something is happening, and you don't know what to do about it.
- A loss can make you focus on the short term and distract you from your long-term plan.

Unexpected negative outcomes can be traumatic as our mind races to figure out what happened, why, what it means and what to do about it.

Who to blame?

Understanding why you lost money can also be complicated:

- Is it someone else's fault?
- Did I trust the wrong information?
- Why didn't someone tell me I could lose money?
- What should I do now?
- How do I recover my losses?
- Will the investment recover and, if so, when?

Unfortunately, investing gets infinitely more complicated when one experiences a loss.

There is nothing simple about losing money except the ability to do it!

FOUR INVESTMENT QUESTIONS

There are four personally relevant questions I recommend investors consider. These four questions are a result of decades of teaching and collaborating with my clients:

1) Why are you investing?
2) Where do returns come from?
3) What is risk?
4) How does one capture return and manage risk?

Let's go through these questions in more detail and look at possible answers.

1) WHY ARE YOU INVESTING?

Many answers may come to mind—investing is a personal decision—but at the most fundamental level, these reasons include:

- I want to.
- I need to.
- I was told to.
- It is the right thing to do.
- I want to get rich or richer.

The primary reason you are investing is to **achieve a return.**

2) WHERE DO RETURNS COME FROM?

There are many answers that come to mind:

- Buying and selling investments
- Picking good investments
- Investing in great companies
- My advisor's instincts

The fundamental source of return is the compensation for **accepting risk**.

3) WHAT IS RISK?

Risk and return have a complicated relationship which can be the cause of many investment problems. Risk, the origin of return, will be discussed throughout the book.

> "**Risk means the chance of being wrong—not always in an adverse direction, but always in a direction different from what we expected.**"
> —Peter Bernstein

Risk, in the simplest form, **is the possibility or probability the expected outcome does not occur**. If you understand, consider the implications, and respect risk, you are better equipped to extract the return.

4) HOW DOES ONE CAPTURE RETURN AND MANAGE RISK?

We seek return, relative to risk, in almost everything we do, from driving a car, to traveling to a foreign country, or attending a rock concert, and so on. We manage the risk by having a plan to manage the variables we control. Investing is no different. The returns we seek are the by-product of risk. We need to focus on processes to manage this risk so we can capture or achieve the intended outcome. Investment return can be captured, and risk better managed, with a rules-based systematic process and structure focusing on the variables we *can* control to better manage the variables we cannot control.

> "Sometimes in life, it's not developing the best answers, but developing the right questions."
> —David Booth

GIVE UP SOMETHING TO GET SOMETHING

Investors want to be right! The simple answer, in the complex world of psychology, is that we want to be right more often than we are wrong. In fact, we hate being wrong way more than we feel good about being right. Investors want, regardless of the natural uncertainty of investing, to be more certain in their approach to investing. They want less cost, they want to pay less in taxes, and they want to avoid losses. Investors want more return with less risk, and they want to believe they can predict and profit from their expectations.

Life, like investing, is a compromise of giving up something to get something. To earn a higher income, we devote years of our life to education. Entrepreneurs work long days to build their businesses. To maintain our health, we make dietary sacrifices and endure hours of weekly exercise. We accept these trade-offs as we appreciate the benefits.

The basis of all investment decisions is the trade-off between risk and return

Successful long-term investing is a trade-off. The dilemma is: what are we willing to give up to get what we want? Do we understand the consequences of what we are giving up to get what we want? Investors need to find an alignment of what they want, what they need, and what they can achieve. In a world where instant gratification is almost demanded, we can lose sight of how risk and return are related. Investors need to understand, accept, and manage the risks that are the source of the long-term returns they seek.

What the investor needs is a rules-based, systematic investment process and structure. This approach will provide clarity, reduce the impact of investment noise, and facilitate better decision-making and analysis. This approach will keep you focused on your goal of capturing returns and managing risks. The approach will enhance consistency and reliability of returns to improve long-term financial planning. You need to appreciate that investing is a game of uncertainty, best managed with patience and intelligence, over a long period of time.

> "You can't always get what you want. But if you try sometimes, you just might find you get what you need."
> —Mick Jagger / Keith Richards

MATH AND EMOTION

Many decisions, including investment decisions, boil down to a choice between math and emotion. When deciding between two options, you can run the numbers and weigh the pros and cons of what to do next. However, even while knowing the math, some people choose to ignore the numbers, and make decisions based on intuition and emotion.

We are, without a doubt, emotional beings, and this can affect short-term thinking. The dilemma is the noise and the emotion of today competes with the long-term strategy for tomorrow. A good example is diet and exercise. Many of us will set up a strategy in the New Year to get in shape and eat better. This strategy may last for weeks, or even months, but eventually procrastination, distraction, and life may get in the way. The math is compelling. Eating better and exercising more will improve the odds of a better quality of life. Why is something so obvious so hard to commit to?

> **Portfolio Investing is math and emotion.**
> **Math is how you should build and structure a portfolio.**
> **Emotion is why you don't.**

Investing suffers from a similar push and pull between what we want to do versus what we should do. It is a psychological battle between what makes us feel good in the moment versus what is good for us over time. The math is the application and process of data to shift the long-term odds in our favor. Emotion is how we feel about it.

Dreams don't pay for retirement, capturing return and managing risk does.

INFORMATION / KNOWLEDGE / WISDOM

Investment information can be like Pandora's box. As we seek out investment ideas and opinions, we may be influenced by incomplete information that can cause more harm than good. There is no shortage of opinions and information on every aspect of investing. All this random data can evoke an emotional response that may lead us to make the wrong decision. Our unchecked curiosity, fear, and greed, and the accessibility and ease of investing in anything, at any time, can increase the risks.

Information is endless and everywhere. We use information as a base for our decisions. The validity of the information and the ability to use it productively can be in question. Knowledge is the collection of information into organized thoughts or processes. The more evidence-based the information, the more valuable the knowledge becomes.

Problems are not solved because someone thinks they are right. Problems are solved with evidence-based substance that rational people can understand and agree on.

Wisdom can improve judgment and decision-making. It is an intangible quality gained through our experiences in life. The primary difference between wisdom and knowledge is that wisdom involves a healthy dose of perspective and the ability to make sound judgments about a subject, while knowledge is simply facts. Anyone can become knowledgeable about a subject by reading, researching, and memorizing facts. Wisdom is understanding when and how to apply knowledge.

> **"Knowledge is being aware of what you can do. Wisdom is knowing when not to do it."**
> **—Anonymous**

Wisdom and knowledge can lead to a better understanding of how to capture investment returns and manage risk. Wisdom and knowledge are critical components of developing and executing an investment strategy aimed to improve long-term odds of investment success.

A TALE OF TWO INVESTORS

As you read this book, I want you to imagine that you are sitting in your favorite coffee shop at ten on a Tuesday morning. There are two individuals sitting at tables, one to your left and one to your right. We will refer to them as **Investor #1** and **Investor #2**. The investors do not know each other but are identical in every way. Same age, same net worth, same education, and most importantly, they have the same investment objectives and constraints. Their underlying goal is to seek out return and grow their wealth.

Investor #1 has read *7 Steps to a Better Portfolio*. She has built and maintained, over the long-term, a rules-based systematic portfolio process and structure based on the 7 Steps.

Investor #2 has not read *7 Steps to a Better Portfolio*.

We will revisit **Investor #1** and **Investor #2** at the end of this book.

7 STEPS TO A BETTER PORTFOLIO

The foundation of *7 Steps to a Better Portfolio* is derived from a student project in one of my finance classes. Students were required to examine some of the investment portfolios from a sampling of British Columbia public pension plans and then answer five questions:

1) How do they allocate their assets?
2) How do they capture returns?
3) How do they manage risk?
4) What do you like about their investment approach?
5) What could they improve on in their investment approach?

Over time, the focus of this exercise shifted toward retail investment management, and the questions evolved into the 7 Steps.

7 STEPS:
1) **Allocate across global capital markets**
2) **Diversify broadly within markets**
3) **Focus on higher expected returns**
4) **Utilize financial science**
5) **Manage strategy risk**
6) **Manage investment choice risk**
7) **Manage costs and taxes**

The 7 Steps are not complicated concepts. Many, on their own, are universally accepted as foundations for a good portfolio approach. Combining the steps will help you navigate through the chaotic world of investment noise, opinions, investment choices, and investment questions. The more informed the investment decision-making, the better the odds of a successful outcome.

The 7 Steps are referenced throughout this book. A detailed explanation of each of the steps can be found in chapter 9. The Steps are then further evaluated relative to three portfolio approaches in chapter 10.

Pension-style portfolio

"Pension-style portfolio" is a term I use throughout the book to define a rules and evidence-based long-term portfolio approach. This type of portfolio is allocated and diversified in a similar fashion to that of a large, institutional pension plan. Investors choose this style of portfolio management to plan for future cash flows and to increase the reliability and consistency of returns to support their long-range financial planning scenarios. "Pension-style investors" are pragmatic thinkers and are ideally suited to utilizing the 7 Steps for their portfolios.

STRUCTURE / STRUCTURE / STRUCTURE

You live in the present and invest today to capture future returns while managing the risks that accompany these returns—for a future that is equally unknown for all investors involved. 7 Steps, designed to capture returns while managing risks, can be summarized in what I refer to as:

Structure/Structure/Structure

- **Structure**: Global allocation across, and broad diversification within, capital markets:
    - Step 1: Allocate across global capital markets
    - Step 2: Diversify broadly within markets
- **Structure:** Investment approach grounded in economic theory and backed by decades of empirical research:
    - Step 3: Focus on higher expected returns
    - Step 4: Utilize financial science
- **Structure:** Manage strategy, investment risks, and costs:
    - Step 5: Manage strategy risk
    - Step 6: Manage investment choice risk
    - Step 7: Manage costs and taxes

Structure/Structure/Structure—The foundation of a great portfolio!

RISK—NOT TOO LITTLE, NOT TOO MUCH

Investing, as will be discussed throughout the book, is about capturing return and managing risk. Risk, the origin of return, should be understood and respected by the investor. Imagine you are investing your life savings for the next ten plus years. Which of these three phrases best reflect your investment philosophy?

- **"Better safe than sorry."** This may imply accepting too little risk and may reduce your odds of long-term investment success
- **"You only live once."** This may imply accepting too much risk and may reduce your odds of long-term investment success.
- **"Watch your step."** This implies accepting the right amount of risk using calculated and controlled steps to improve your odds of long-term investment success.

Risk is inseparable from return. *7 Steps* focuses on what investors can control to better manage what they can't.

IT DOES NOT MATTER WHAT ANYONE ELSE DOES; IT MATTERS WHAT YOU DO

In our "comparative" society, you may be concerned about what everyone else is doing. You see, or assume, that someone you know is getting rich off tech stocks, oil stocks, or Bitcoins, and so on. You should be happy for them. They chose to make the investment, took the risks, and achieved success.

Everyone seems to have the answers to others' problems

There is no shortage of friends, family, coworkers, media, and advisors willing to tell you how they invest or how you should invest your money. The problem is that these folks are not going to pay for your retirement, you are.

It does not matter how anyone else manages their portfolio; it matters what you do. What you do is utilize a rules-based systematic investment process and structure to improve your odds of long-term investment success.

Odds are everything!
Managing the variables to improve the odds is everything else!

Successful long-term investing is about you, your investments, your investment strategy, and the odds. You must understand yourself and how you react to, manage, and interpret information in the uncertain world of investing.

Odds favor the informed and the disciplined

You have a responsibility to make informed decisions when you invest your money. Successful long-term investing will be determined by the quality of your decisions and the framework or structure with which you evaluate those decisions. The quality of your decisions will depend on what information is evidence based and what is opinion based. An intelligently structured and disciplined portfolio approach will provide consistency, help you manage variables, and reduce the impact of investment noise. The goal is to keep you focused on capturing return and managing risk to enable you to improve your odds of long-term investment success.

TAKEAWAYS:

- Portfolio investing is math and emotion.
- Ask yourself the four questions:
    - Why am I investing?
    - Where do returns come from?
    - What is risk?
    - How do I capture returns and manage risk?
- Successful long-term investing is about you, your investments, your investment strategy, and the odds.
- Understand what you can control to better manage what you cannot control.

Chapter 2

Investment Journey

Investing is a journey into the uncertainty of tomorrow

Investing is the journey into uncertainty, of you and your savings, relative to a series of decisions around risk, return, time, and odds. How you perceive risk and return will be affected by your investment personality, financial situation, motivation, education, prior experience, and the quality of advice and information you receive. The investing journey, as expected, is full of characters with diverse opinions and motives. You are tasked with the difficult job of evaluating the reliability and relevance of endless information.

History painfully documents the harsh truths of investing

Investing is complicated and full of uncertainty and noise. No investor gets by unscathed. When you're old enough to realize you have made mistakes, one can hope you're young enough to learn from them.

> "As humans, we subconsciously tend to focus only on the bad, overlooking or completely dismissing what went right."
> —Byron Morrison

Time is constant, markets are not

Time is a constant to everyone reading this book. We will all, barring death, be ten years older ten years from now. It is an absolute and is equal for all. The question becomes, did you put in the effort to utilize better information, make good decisions, and get the most benefit over this journey of time? Markets are not constant. Markets are an ever-evolving, asset-pricing mechanism impacted by participants' views of new information. Markets and investing are complicated, full of uncertainty and noise. Markets, an investment fund, or a specific stock, may rise or fall at any time, creating euphoria, fear, panic, or indifference. Meanwhile the media, social media, and social circles contribute to shifting feelings of uncertainty and optimism.

Investing can be frustrating

Investing can be a frustrating experience. What seems easy and makes sense when markets are rising can become complicated and uncertain when markets and investments fall. Investing in ever evolving markets was never easy.

EXAMPLE 2.1: INVESTING GIVETH AND INVESTING TAKETH AWAY

Investing returns can feel surreal as portfolio values rise and fall. Imagine that, on March 1, you have an investment portfolio worth $500,000.

Scenario 1: It's now November 1, seven months later, and your portfolio is worth $560,000. You did not do anything, and your net portfolio worth increased by $60,000. In addition to feeling fairly good about the current situation, you might ask, "Where did I get this additional wealth?"

Scenario 2: It's now November 1, seven months later, and your portfolio is worth $440,000. Last March, when the portfolio was at $500,000, you were thinking of, but did not buy, a $60,000 power boat to cruise around Vancouver Island, British Columbia (BC). Today, November 1, your portfolio is worth $440,000, and you did not buy a boat. Not only do you feel uncomfortable about the current risk the market is experiencing, but you might also think to yourself, "Where is the boat I never owned?"

Losses are not just words or numbers on a page. Losses and declining asset prices are real and can create financial hardship and emotional insecurity. Losses and feeling uncertain can be very unnerving.

OPPORTUNITY COST AND DECISION-MAKING

If I offered you $100,000 today, or $100,000 a year from now, which would you choose? The logical person would, of course, select the $100,000 today, because you would not have to wait.

But what if I offered you $100,000 today or $110,000 in a year?

The decision becomes more difficult. If you took $100,000 today, you would need to earn (using simple math) a 10 percent return on the money to end up with $110,000 in one year. If you thought you could make a higher return, you would take the money now. If you did not think this was realistic, waiting one year for the money might make more sense.

This is a classic example of opportunity cost. Opportunity cost is the forgone benefit that would have been derived from an option not chosen. Making informed, logical, rational investment evaluations will help you understand the risks, the odds, and the opportunity costs, and will improve your decision-making processes.

INVESTOR PERSONALITIES AND INVESTMENT STRUCTURES

Along the investment journey, you will not only experience your own learning curve, but you may come across a variety of other investment personalities and investment approaches.

Investment personalities

Investors exhibit a broad range of personalities when tasked with investment decisions. Their personalities are shaped by both their own innate nature and their exposures to historical experiences. Investors, it has been said, rely more on intuition, rather than logic and process. In my thirty years in the industry, I have witnessed a broad range of investment personalities.

Confirmation Cathy seeks out only advice that confirms her views. Whether it is pessimism or optimism, this type of investor lacks objectivity.

Fear-mongering Frank is dangerous. Fear mongering is an attempt to destabilize logical and rational thoughts with low probability outcomes or conspiracy theories that create insecurity and confusion. This problem has been called psychological warfare. To counter the fear-mongers, one should use simple statistics. Anything is possible, but is it probable? We live most of our lives in the 99.99 percent probability range. Fear-mongering Frank is likely wrong again.

FOMO Fred has a Fear of Missing Out. He may seek guidance from the media, investment blogs, and gurus. Fred wants what the winners have.

Go-along Greg is a combination of too trusting, too naïve, and indifferent. Investors like Greg must be reminded to remember they are not buying a microwave or ordering a pizza; they are investing their assets to attain a return that will pay for their retirement.

MEME Michael thinks online chat forums like Reddit constitute investment advice. Just because a MEME stock can gain a cult-like following on social media platforms does not in any way suggest it is a prudent investment choice. A MEME is defined as an amusing or interesting item that is spread widely online through social media.

Naïve Nate is the kind of investor that jumps on his friend's motorbike without any experience or training because "it seemed like a good idea at the time." Naïve investors don't want to know, don't understand, or simply are not concerned with investing risk until it's too late.

Nervous Nancy worries when markets go up and gets even more scared when markets go down. This type of investor is generally a nervous person. She may have fear or a lack of clarity, or she may mistrust investing. Nancy may "cry wolf" when she sees the neighbor's dog. The downside is that she may miss capturing the returns of the global capital markets over her investing time frame.

Positive Penny is too optimistic. She may be a poor judge of risk. Penny is hopeful that investments always go up. She may misunderstand or ignore risks and may lack perspective. Big wins may be overshadowed by some big losses.

Rational Roger is pragmatic and realistic. He thinks things through and has the self-control to minimize emotional decision-making. Roger is less focused on predictions and more focused on investment processes and structure. He understands that markets evolve with changing perceptions and knows how risk and return are related. Roger's portfolio is prudently allocated and broadly diversified.

Trader Tom likes the thrill of the trade. Tom is an opportunistic-driven investor looking for a trading or investing edge. He may be a follower of stock charts, chat rooms, and trading patterns. Tom is seeking a quick return because he believes he is right. He wants, needs, and thinks he deserves his trade going in the right direction.

Ask the questions

Regardless of investment personality type and outside influences, investors should have a clear understanding of what their investment approach is, why the approach is good for their situation, and most importantly, why this approach places the long-term odds of investment success in their favor.

Like gaming and lotteries, some of the investors noted above may hit a streak of luck. This may mislead others to think predicting and investing is easy. Winning feels easy when you win. Planning to win, which is not as easy, is about investment process, structure, and the odds.

Investment portfolio structures

Investors may utilize various portfolio structures to accomplish their objective. Over my years in the industry, I have seen many portfolios cross my desk. Most portfolios are either concentrated or hold a mixed bag of assorted investments. Remember a portfolio adds up to 100 percent and each component of the portfolio has a role to play to improve the odds of long-term investment success.

Concentrated portfolios are a selection of one's high-conviction investments. The focus is on return and with less concern or understanding of risk.

Mixed bag is the most common portfolio structure. It's a portfolio of assorted funds, stocks, exchange-traded funds, and bonds. The investor may hold many highly correlated assets and may not be aware of the risks.

Globally allocated, broadly diversified portfolio. Although these are rare, these portfolios are designed like personal pension plans for the "Rational Rogers" of the investing world. I will discuss the benefits of this structure throughout this book, with the goal of convincing you that you should learn to be a "Rational Roger."

FOUR QUADRANTS TO INVESTMENT DECISION-MAKING

Investors will approach investment decision-making with a variety of different perspectives. Using the quadrant approach helps to generalize what drives investors to make investment decisions.

NOISE TRADING

The Noise quadrant is composed of investors who believe in both market timing and stock selection. They think they or their favorite guru can consistently uncover mispriced securities that will deliver market-beating returns. In addition, they believe it is possible to identify the mispricing of an entire market and predict when it will turn up or down. The reality is that most of these methods fail to even match the market, let alone beat it. Unfortunately, most of the "do it yourself investors" fall into this quadrant and much of the media plays into this thinking.

CONVENTIONAL BUY AND HOLD STOCK STRATEGY

This strategy includes most of the financial services industry. Most investment professionals have the experience to know that they cannot predict broad market swings with any degree of accuracy. However, they believe their thousands of market analysts and portfolio managers can find undervalued securities for their customers. However, in an efficient capital market, this methodology adds no value on average. It's simply great marketing.

FORECASTERS AND MARKET TIMERS

Investors in this quadrant believe that even though individual securities are priced efficiently, they can find broad mispricing in entire market sectors. They think they can add value by buying when a market is undervalued, waiting until the rest of the investors finally recognize their mistake, then selling when the market is fairly valued once again. It is inconsistent to think that individual securities are priced fairly, but that entire markets, which are aggregates of the priced individual securities, are not. More great marketing.

ACADEMICS, INSTITUTIONAL PLANS, AND *7 STEPS TO A BETTER PORTFOLIO*

This is where most of the academic community resides, as well as most large North American pension and endowment plans. Investors in this quadrant dispassionately research what works and then follow a rational course of action, based on empirical evidence rather than marketing.

Figure 2.1: Four quadrants to investment decision making

	Market timing	No market timing
Stock selection	Noise trading	Conventional buy and hold stock strategy
No stock selection	Forecasters Market timers	Academia *7 Steps to a Better Portfolio*

OPINIONS AND FORECASTS

Opinions play a significant role in the investment process. We cannot help giving our opinion on investing, sports, politics, other drivers, and so on. It's human nature to have an opinion. Opinions are views or judgments and are not necessarily based on knowledge or facts.

Each January, at the annual Victoria Chartered Financial Analysts (CFA) forecasting dinner, two or more guest speakers will explain the past, talk about the present, forecast the future of the markets, and designate their favorite stock picks. Each of us in the audience can also participate by writing down our forecasted one-year expected value of the S&P TSX (Canadian stock market), the S&P 500 (US stock market), the Canadian dollar, and price of oil in USD.

> "Forecasts may tell you a great deal about the forecaster; they tell you nothing about the future."
> —Warren Buffett

Investors interpret and use opinions and forecasts differently, depending on their prior knowledge, interest in the subject, personal motivation, and beliefs. We seek authoritative and confident voices (in politics, sports, or investing) that, regardless of their predictive abilities, tells us what we hope to hear. The predictors become legendary when they are correct and make acceptable excuses when they are wrong.

Forecasts play a significant role in asset pricing and risk management. Overly confident or stretched forecasts may give us a false sense of security, causing us to take ill-advised risks.

Investors tend to look for confirmation of their belief systems in the media, and often close their minds to things that might invalidate their beliefs. Herd mentality and overly optimistic estimates of future outcomes can pose a significant risk to the unsuspecting investor. We can be misled to believe things we want to believe. When a vocal majority believes something will happen, even if the odds suggest it will not, it can create significant price risk for some investments. You can see the cheerleaders in the media saying, "it's different this time." It may seem different, but the math is always the same. Over-hyped expensive stocks do not go up forever. They never have, and never will. Valuation issues, like gravity, eventually catch up.

> "'This time is different' are among the most costly four words in market history."
> —Sir John Templeton

Everyone has their opinions and often speak with such authority that we forget that many opinions are not based on facts. The fact that someone says something with authority does not mean it is rooted in knowledge. We must look beyond the convincing passion and presentation of information to determine whether it is based on objective information. The more we believe in something, the more enthusiastic we become. More enthusiasm for something does not imply it is the correct answer.

At any time, you can find someone on social media screaming, "The markets are going to crash" or "This stock will go up 200 percent." They do so with such conviction and passion, it is disturbing.

Hearing and reading about endless forecasts and opinions is not the problem. The problem is how do we filter and process these opinions and use them to our advantage? The solution is to have a rules-based, systematic investment process and a structure to assess the risk and the relevance of the information.

> "The problem with the world is that the intelligent people are full of doubts, while the stupid ones are full of confidence."
> —Charles Bukowski

INFORMATION CAROUSEL

Markets are moved by investors' perceptions on the news. News, by definition, is new information. This new information, which competes for our attention, arrives randomly from many sources. This information, as received and understood, may have an impact on our understanding of risk and return.

An example is the story carousel exercise you may remember from grade school. Assume we have fifteen people sitting in a circle. Each person can talk to one person on their left and one their right. Person #1 tells the person to their right, person #2, a story (new information) and then person #2 passes that story on to person #3. This continues around the circle, until it gets to person #15 at which time they tell the story, as they understand it, to the whole group. This story may or may not be factually correct.

Investors crave a story to explain an event. The story can take on a life of its own regardless of the accuracy.

Information in the form of a story can be interpreted differently by the listener, depending on their concentration, understanding, and interest in the story. This can lead to simple misunderstanding of the story and can affect the integrity of the story elements.

Misinformation is incorrect or misleading information presented as fact, either intentionally or unintentionally. Investment messenger boards on various social media platforms may contain this type of misleading information. This can be very harmful to your perceptions of expected risks and returns.

There is nothing like the power of a story. Even if it's unsubstantiated, contains bad advice, and is misleading. An uncomfortable term that gained attention this past decade is "fake news." Crazy predictions, of which there is no shortage, based on distorted or false information, can wreak havoc on investment decision making.

> "Beliefs do not make something true. Just because you claim to think something is true does not make it true."
> —Judge Maya Gamble

The more exaggerated the claim, the more the messenger fears being exposed, and the more convinced they must be right.

Conspiracy theories are a dangerous form of misinformation. With the internet, there is an opportunity for participants to make any unproven claim they feel like making. There are numerous conspiracy stories based on unsubstantiated claims in the areas of finance, medicine, and politics. The original author may not check the facts or provide evidence-based reference notes. Think of it as handing in a term paper in school with completely made-up claims and no creditable references. This would never be accepted in any standard educational setting. Unfortunately, it is accepted as valid to some people reading social media posts. There is no evidence these unfounded claims hold truth, just the minority group of less informed readers who think, and will tell others, that it is true. You should, as should everyone, maintain a healthy focus on evidence-based reality and logical perspective relating to science, finance, history, and common law.

INFLUENCERS ARE NOT EXPERTS

A recent example of influence can be found in the growth of sports betting. Recently BETMGM launched a new sports betting website for Canadian residents. It is commonly known in sports betting and casino gambling that the house or the bookie has the best odds of making the money. Meyer Lansky, a famous gangster from the 1920s to the 1970s, knew the sports bettor or gambler seeks out the opportunistic excitement of the win, but the odds were stacked against them. He knew that gamblers are not rational, and they live in the moment; they can be emotionally tricked into believing they can outperform the other side of the bet, to win more than they lose. Lansky was a pioneer of today's sports and casino betting.

BETMGM launched in Canada in the 2021 with a television commercial featuring hockey legend Wayne Gretzky. Wayne says with great authority: "With every tap a new legend is born. A chance to grab destiny. Defy the odds and strike. Because every bet with BETMGM has a potential for greatness," at which point in the commercial, it shows an index finger tapping on a $100 bet.

Wayne, what are you doing in the commercial? Why are you influencing folks to gamble? You are the best hockey player in history. What is your experience with online gaming? Does anyone really need to bet $100 on the outcome of tonight's sporting event? Do the people you are influencing understand the risks of gambling? You cannot fault BETMGM, as they know, as did Meyer Lansky, that entertainment and celebrities draw in the gamblers.

> "A gambler is nothing but a man who makes a living out of false hopes."
> —William Bolitho

There is a strange irony with this influencer. In 2006, Wayne and his wife Janet Jones were caught being associated with, but not guilty of, a crime related to a nationwide gambling ring with ties to then Phoenix Coyotes' assistant coach Rick Tocchet. The investigation was dubbed "Operation Slap Shot" by the authorities. Janet Jones, according to the ESPN report, dated February 9, 2006, was quoted as saying, "At no time did I ever place a wager on my husband's behalf. Other than the occasional horse race, my husband does not bet on any sports."

Just because you can invest in almost anything at anytime does not suggest it is a good idea

Sports betting can be compared to stock trading. You want to be on the right side of the bet. Like sports betting, investors may not be aware of, or care about, the risks or the odds of the return relative to the risk. Sports bettors, day traders, and market timers think they have control. They may think they have control because they have choices over their bets. The real control is understanding the big picture and the long-term odds. I would bet a Diet Coke that Wayne Gretzky made more money doing the BETMGM commercial than he did betting on sports. If you want a reflective perspective of the odds of sports betting and gambling, research hall-of-fame-golfer Phil Mickelson.

> "My gambling got to the point of reckless and embarrassing"
> —Phil Mickelson

Before you get bamboozled by an influencer, find out if they have the education, experience, and knowledge of the subject they are promoting.

EXTREME VIEWS DRIVE FEAR, GREED, AND CURIOSITY

Extreme views are headline grabbers:

- The stock market is headed for a 50% crash!
- This stock is the next Amazon!
- Gold will be $5,000 per ounce by the end of this year!
- Oil will go to $10 a barrel!
- Meet the next Warren Buffet!
- Bigfoot spotted in Florida!

Is it possible or probable? Anything is possible, it's just not probable

Anything is possible. But you should ask yourself: is it probable? If it helps, you should also ask yourself: is it relevant to your life and objectives? When Will Smith slapped Chris Rock at the Oscars in 2022, there was a story circulating that it was all staged. I do not know if it was staged; however, the odds, based on the facts, suggest that it was not. The event is also not relevant to your life. In the noisy social media world, one must be careful not to fall for extreme views. We can lead a more productive and happier life when we evaluate other views relative to relevance and probability. It can be as simple as asking ourselves, or persons with objective knowledge, what are the odds a given story is or will turn out to be correct, and is it relevant to my objectives? You are likely to improve your decision-making process by making rational logical decisions based on evidence-based information. You are likely to stay more focused on your objective if you ignore irrelevant noise. Focus on what is probable rather than outliers that are possible.

Don't be fooled by the messengers of greed and fear.

EXAMPLE 2.2: SAMPLE OF ACTUAL EMAIL SENT TO THE AUTHOR

I received this email on Sunday, October 16, 2022.

Note: I did not subscribe to this email list, and I have no idea how I got on the list. It is a good example of information that motivates with greed and fear

Dear Subscriber,

Every day the media opens up a fire hydrant of bad news . . . and we get soaked.

War. Inflation. Tanking markets. The housing market turning from Boom to Bust . . .

No wonder most investors are spooked.

But there's a group of investors who—amidst all this bad news—are smiling because they are profiting from it. *How? By using a special category of defensive investments to flip every crisis into a profit opportunity.*

With one of these, investors could have made average gains of **126%** *with no losers, even as the stock market was falling. That's not a typo. I mean ZERO losers.*

In another category, they spotted 62 different defensive investment opportunities for "crash days" in the market. And sure enough, on one crash day this year, they saw average gains of **206%***. On a second crash day, they saw average gains of* **251%***.*

And on a third crash day, ***the average gains were 324%.*** *Per day. Dr. "X" just laid out how it all works in a critically timed briefing on the Collapse of 2022/2023. Many investors could be devastated in the months ahead.*

But you don't have to be one of them. Watch Dr. X's time-sensitive briefing while time is still on your side.

Best,

I changed the name to Dr. X because I don't want to get sued by the sender of the email.

The odds the email claim is real are the same as the odds that Big Foot lives in Florida. It's not impossible; it's just highly improbable.

AVOID DOOM SCROLLING

The term "doom scrolling" became popular during the COVID-19 pandemic. The term is described as the tendency to continue to seek out or consume predominantly bad news. As this news can be saddening, disheartening, or depressing, it can be harmful to decision-making. Social media algorithms heed the content user's engagement, which amplifies its intensity. The content lacks objectivity and feeds one's insecurities or fear.

MANAGE INFORMATION AND REDUCE MISTAKES

"Do you really want to invest your hard-earned savings—the money you'll need for your kids' college or your own retirement—based on someone's hunch or wish?"
—David Booth

Your investment journey is full of questions, investment styles, personalities, approaches, opinions, forecasts, and endless information, all of which are subject to interpretation errors. All of these can be distracting and confusing, and cause errors in judgment and decision-making. You are going to make mistakes over your investing journey by accident; do not make any on purpose.

When Jason Zweig, a columnist at *The Wall Street Journal*, asked Daniel Kahneman if the opposite of "noise" is "quiet," he said, **"No: The opposite of noise is discipline. It's doing things in a reasoned way, organizing your thinking so it is as intentional as possible."**

What are you trying to accomplish when you invest and put your investments at risk? Is your investment thesis based on hope or evidence-based logic? No matter how crazy the investment world may appear at times, never forget why you are investing. Ask yourself the four questions:

1) Why am I investing?
2) Where do returns come from?
3) What is risk?
4) How do I capture returns and manage risks?

A rules-based, systematic investment process and structure will help you manage information flow to keep you focused on your goal of capturing return and managing risk over your investment horizon.

TAKEAWAYS:

- Investing is a journey into uncertainty.
- Investors' personalities will affect how they evaluate investing risk.
- Utilize objective and credible information sourced from reputable publishing sources.
- Manage how information affects your decision-making.

Chapter 3
Risk and Return

Investing risk is inseparable from return

You will encounter many different types of risks along your investment journey. The primary risk most applicable for the purposes of this book is the risk that the actual return on an investment will be different from its expected return. For example, assume that you expect a 10 percent return but receive minus 2 percent. The uncertainty of outcomes is critical to understanding risk and return. If there was no uncertainty, then the investment return would be risk-free, nonexistent returns.

Risk, the origin of return, is seldom understood

The basis of all investment decisions is the trade-off between risk and return. Unfortunately, at any point in time, people tend to focus on only one of the "Rs." When times are good, nobody thinks about risk; when times are bad, people think only about risks—and the truth lies somewhere between.

> "One of the cornerstones of modern finance is the nexus of return and risk. These two characteristics are joined at the hip—you simply don't get one without the other."
> —William Bernstein

Investing risk can be hard to grasp. You may not be able to see it, feel it, or understand it. But risk is always there. Risk is fundamental to investment returns. Investors must constantly be aware of the risks they are assuming, understand them, and be prepared for the emotional and financial consequences.

Another underlying risk that will be discussed throughout this book is commonly referred to as "influence risk." Influence risk is different than investing risk in that there is no trade-off of compensating return. Influence risk is simply basing your decisions on bad advice. Media, social media, or social circles can make investors believe something that is highly improbable to be true. It's a pervasive risk in many aspects of society. With investing, it can lead investors to ignore evidence-based research and misinterpret financial risks and odds.

RISK—THE PAST, PRESENT, AND FUTURE

Past risk is often measured as the up and down price movement, or volatility, of a given market or specific investment. Past risk may be easy to visualize on a chart and, with historical context and hindsight, can be reasonably understood and rationalized. Rationalizing past risks may create a false sense of security when evaluating current and future risks.

Current risk is happening now and you're not sure what to do about it. Current risk can be the most dangerous and often the least understood. Risk is the uncertainty of the future; the more unpleasant the current situation, the more heightened the level of fear of the future. Current risk may require decisions that can be uncomfortable.

Current risk is palpable uncertainty you feel in your gut.

EXAMPLE 3.1: CURRENT INVESTMENT RISK

Imagine you have a globally diversified portfolio of $1,000,000 on December 31, 2019. In early April 2020, you look at your portfolio statement and its value is now $810,676. Your portfolio has, in three months, declined by $189,324 or 18.93 percent.

What should you do?

This portfolio decline and loss of wealth can be very uncomfortable. The current risk and uncertainty of COVID-19 was very real and financially painful. Uncertainty and volatile markets are part of the investing journey. Remember the four questions from chapter 1:

1) Why am I investing?
2) Where do returns come from?
3) What is risk?
4) How do I capture returns and manage risks?

Risk and the financial impact of risk can appear quickly and unpredictably. You may find more confidence in, and comfort with, a rules-based, systematic portfolio process and structure that is globally allocated and broadly diversified. The more trust and conviction you have in an intelligent investment approach, the better you will weather any current and future economic and financial storms.

> "The stock market is a device for transferring money from the impatient to the patient."
> —Warren Buffett

Future risk is the reason I wrote this book. To worry is human. We must figure out how to use the variables we can control to best mitigate the effects of the variables we can't. Like taking the strategic steps to improve health, get more education, and save more money, these controllable and executable steps can go a long way to improving your odds of a successful outcome. *7 Steps* is about recognizing and understanding important investing issues and decisions that have a relevant impact on the odds of investment outcomes. The steps utilize evidence-based information to help you develop a portfolio process and structure. The objective is to improve your odds of capturing future returns, while managing the future risks that accompany the uncertainty of investing.

You can't predict but you can prepare

INVESTING IS A BET ON A PAYOFF RELATIVE TO A PROBABILITY

Investing is a bet on a payoff relative to a probability. That's it! Never forget that!

The payoff is the return. The probability is the odds of achieving the potential return. The payoff on the bet will depend on the probability of the occurrence of your expected outcome.

Market participants determine the risk based on their perceptions of potential outcomes. Like sports betting, the participants are constantly evaluating new information and updating their bets relative to who they think will win or lose in each situation. A stock that is highly favored by many investors may, by this group, be considered less risky to own. A stock that is not liked by many investors may be considered riskier to own.

EXAMPLE 3.2: THEY WAY WE PERCEIVE RISK WILL HAVE AN IMPACT ON EXPECTED RETURN

You have two uncles; both want to borrow $50,000 from you for one year.

Uncle Bob is your favorite uncle. You decide to lend him the $50,000 at 5 percent as he appears, in your view, to be low risk. You have accepted the 5 percent interest as a trade-off for the perceived risk.

Uncle Steve is your least favorite uncle. He has great enthusiasm that the money you lend him will propel him to a new level of success. You decide to lend him the $50,000 at 10 percent as, in your view, he appears to be riskier than Uncle Bob. You have accepted the 10 percent interest as a trade-off for the perceived risk.

In simple terms, lending money to Uncle Bob is a lower risk proposition. If, however, you lend to Uncle Steve, your payoff—in the form of a higher return—is compensation for accepting more risk. This is a very important relationship in understanding risk, return, and asset pricing. You have determined the rate of interest you would charge, based on your perceived risks. The interest rate is also referred to as the "required rate of return." You require a return of 5 percent to lend to Uncle Bob and a return of 10 percent to lend to Uncle Steve.

The market is a pricing mechanism based on investors' perception of risk and return

In the markets, millions of investors and billions of dollars of trades reflect investors' perceptions of risks and returns. The cumulative trades reflect all the risk investors perceive. Just as you assessed Uncle Bob and Uncle Steve, the markets may assess one company with a risk, or required rate of return, of 5 percent and another with a risk of 10 percent.

Required rates of return and how they affect asset prices and expected returns are very important considerations when building a portfolio. (Please see appendices 2, 3, and 4.)

EXAMPLE 3.3: RISK AND RETURN AND THE LAW OF LARGE NUMBERS

Suppose you were able to find 1,000 folks like Uncle Bob and 1,000 folks like Uncle Steve in example 3.2. You refer to each of the groups as the 1,000 Uncle Bobs and the 1,000 Uncle Steves. As in the prior example, you determined that the Uncle Bobs were a safer bet and you decided to lend to them at 5 percent. In addition, you determined the Uncle Steves were a risky consideration and you lent them funds at 10 percent.

Assume you gave each of the 1000 Uncle Bobs a loan for $10,000 at rate of 5 percent. At the same time, you gave each of the 1,000 Uncle Steves a loan for $10,000 at rate of 10 percent. You made a total of 2,000 loans.

Which group of 1,000 loans may provide the biggest average percent return over the next year?

If most of the Uncle Steves paid off the 10 percent loan in one year, you would be compensated with a higher return for the riskier loans.

This is an example about understanding risk and return and the law of large numbers. I will cover this concept throughout the book and the appendices.

Sorry, not a winner

Payoffs and probabilities can be compared to the odds of winning a lottery. Think of it as possible versus probable. Most people understand the probability, but few want to believe it. It is possible you will win the lottery. It's just not probable that you will. Like playing the lottery, we all want to make the big win. And as with the lottery, some small proportion of investors will experience big wins.

EXAMPLE 3.4: THE PAYOFFS / RETURNS RELATE TO PROBABILITIES

Place an average size wastepaper basket on the floor. Take a pair of rolled up socks and measure four feet, fourteen feet, and twenty-four feet from the wastepaper basket.

- Toss the socks into the basket from **four feet**. Success is possible and probable.
- Toss the socks into the basket from **fourteen feet.** Success is possible, but not as probable as the prior toss.
- Toss the socks into the basket from **twenty-four feet.** Success is possible, but not probable.

The emotional reward for tossing a sock four feet into a wastepaper basket is minimal. The emotional reward of dropping it into the bucket at fourteen feet feels pretty good. The emotional high of sinking the sock shot at twenty-four feet can feel exhilarating.

Risk in investing is not as simple as a game of tossing socks. Understand that return is an expectation, not a guarantee, whether it is a four-, fourteen-, or twenty-four-foot shot. If someone tells you they have a high return investment, make sure you consider the odds of sinking a twenty-four-foot sock toss shot.

EXAMPLE 3.5: BUS / CAR / MOTORCYCLE

Imagine you live in Victoria, BC, and you have a relationship with someone who lives in Parksville, BC. The distance between the two cities is approximately 150 kilometers. Along the route, there is a twenty kilometer stretch of highway referred to as the Malahat, and this section of highway is affected by sudden weather changes. You plan on driving up and back twice a week.

You have three choices of transportation for making the journey:

- Bus
- Car
- Motorcycle

A bus is a good example of low-risk transportation (it is very probable you will reach your destination), and it is low reward. The low reward is that you end up smelling like the bus, and it takes five hours to get from door to door.

A car is a good example of moderate risk and moderate return. You incur the added risk of driving (there is a higher probability of distractions and delays), but the reward is that the trip takes two and a half hours, door to door.

A motorbike is a good example of high risk and high reward. You incur more risk driving a motor bike (more exposure to the weather and less visibility to other vehicles), but the reward is a much speedier trip to get from door to door.

The choice of transportation will depend on each person's objective, and their tolerance for risk.

RISK AND ASSET PRICING

EXAMPLE 3.6: CHANGES IN PERCEIVED RISK CAN AFFECT ASSET PRICING

Changes in risk, perceived or real, can have a direct impact on asset pricing. Imagine you are thinking of buying a rental property for $500,000. You reason, based on rising house prices, that you can sell the property for a good return in a few years.

Before you close the deal to purchase, a motor bike gang sets up a clubhouse in a neighboring home. With this new information and the perceived risk of this new situation, you do not want to pay $500,000. You think $425,000 is a better price as compensation for the added risk and uncertainty. The seller recognizes the risk and drops the price to $475,000.

Now, let's assume there are rumors the city will close the clubhouse due to bylaw infractions. As the perceived risk declines, another potential buyer emerges and offers $450,000 to purchase the house. The asset is priced based on the perceived risks and returns of the buyers and the seller. The actual value of the house is best determined when the buyer and seller agree on a price.

Risk and asset pricing are directly related. In theory, higher risk assets should have lower prices and higher expected returns.

RISK, RETURN, AND THE LAW OF LARGE NUMBERS

The goal of investing is to capture a return. Returns are compensation for risk. It would seem logical that investors accepting higher risk should experience higher returns. The assumption is correct, but the problem lies in a common statistical concept referred to as the "law of large numbers." In probability theory, the law of large numbers refers to performing the same action or experiment a large number of times. The results obtained from a large number of trials should approach the expected value as more trials are conducted. For example, while a casino may lose on a single spin of the roulette wheel, its long-term earnings will tend towards a predictable percentage over a large number of spins. This is the reason the casino is in business; it wins the gamblers' money over time.

The law of large numbers does not guarantee that a given sample, especially a small sample, will reflect the true population characteristics. The law of large numbers, which favors a broadly diversified investment approach over time, plays an important part in portfolio investing.

EXAMPLE 3.7: PORTFOLIOS AND THE LAW OF LARGE NUMBERS

Let's assume you have two portfolios. As a result of an unexpected rise in inflation, the markets have declined and both portfolios are down 15 percent. In this scenario, each portfolio that was worth $1,000,000 now has a market value of $850,000. Let's look at two investing scenarios:

Portfolio 1: A globally allocated and broadly diversified portfolio of index and asset class funds

Portfolio 2: A portfolio of 10 to 30 stocks

The downturn in the market was a result of higher and unexpected risk. The increased risk caused asset values to decline. Over time, as the unexpected risk is better understood, the risks may decrease, and asset prices may increase. The law of large numbers does not guarantee that a given sample, especially a small sample, will reflect the true population characteristics. Guessing which assets will do better than others is very difficult. The portfolio holding a larger number of different stocks—the sample size is larger—will have a higher probability of capturing any future market appreciation. It would make sense to own a broadly diversified portfolio of 1,000 global assets (large data sample) to capture the returns. The odds, as for the casinos, are in your favor. Of course, there is always a chance that with only a few holdings you could have a massive positive return. That is entirely possible but is not probable.

BEAR MARKETS AND HIGHER EXPECTED RETURNS

It's called a "bear market" when a market experiences a major market decline of 20 percent or more amid widespread pessimism and negative investor sentiment. Bear markets may be caused by increased risks that may include a weak or sluggish economy, the bursting of a speculative bubble, a pandemic, or geopolitical crises.

The problem with bear markets is predicting the depth and duration of the declining market. The benefits of bear markets are the lower-priced assets, and the current high risks create higher expected returns going forward. In the evolution of capitalism, there will be companies that succeed and companies that fail. There will always be smart and skilled entrepreneurs that come up with new and better products to fill the ever-growing global demand.

EXAMPLE 3.8: ASSET PRICING AND RISK (EXPECTED RETURN)

In example 3.2, you estimated the risks and required returns of lending funds to Uncle Bob at 5 percent and Uncle Steve at 10 percent. You expected a higher return if you lent funds to Uncle Steve, as a compensation for the higher associated risks.

Referring to example 3.6, and the arrival of risk (the motorcycle gang) in your neighborhood, the unexpected occurrence and the resulting risk caused asset prices to decline.

Assume that on January 15, a globally allocated, broadly diversified portfolio was worth $1,000,000. The expected return (risk) for a portfolio of investments was 7 percent over the coming years. Then over the next few months, new information about a rapid increase in unexpected global inflation causes the portfolio to decline by 20 percent. Risk rises and asset prices fall.

However, as risk rises, so does expected return. This implies that the current expected return on the $800,000 is likely much greater than the 7 percent estimated when prices were higher, and risks were lower.

One of two things can happen:

1) The increase in risk (uncertainty) can scare off investors; they sell and leave the stock market. They may believe the market will get worse and more unexpected bad news will arrive, driving up the risk and driving down the asset values. This may very well happen, as we recognize the future is unknown.
2) The increase in risk (uncertainty) can be seen as an opportunity with the expectation of higher future returns. We do know that higher risk and lower asset prices translates to higher expected returns.

The irony is that the portfolio, which may not have hit bottom yet, should have mathematically higher returns over the next 1, 3, and 5 years as of July 15 than it did on January 15.

UNDERSTANDING FEAR AND RISK

Many years ago, when I was on an Alaska cruise, I did a zip-line excursion. Somehow, when signing up while on the comfy confines of the ship, I forgot about my fear of heights and never considered how high up in the trees the zip lines would be. After we walked up to the first platform, my enthusiasm for the excursion turned to heightened anxiety. At this point, my emotions required management by my logical brain. I had to understand what was going to happen and trust that the operators knew what they were doing.

To worry is risk management

There is nothing wrong with fear itself. Fear is a great emotional protector—your brain is telling you to be more careful. Fear makes sure you put in precautions to protect yourself. And once I understood what the zip-line adventure involved and trusted the process, I could manage the fear. My fear was managed with the use of securely fastened harnesses, and the capable and respectful zip-line staff members.

Similarly, everyone should be fearful of risky investments and risky investing plans, no matter how cool they sound. *7 Steps* is a portfolio process and structure that, once you understand and trust it, will help you manage your fears of investing and keep you on track to get you down the line.

LADDER OF EXPECTED RETURNS AND RISKS

All investments fall into a general category that can be sorted into expected returns and risks.

Different types of investment vehicles have different expected risks and returns. Think of a ladder that you are using to access apples in a tree. Each step up the ladder offers a trade-off between the risks on the ladder in exchange for more apples. As you go up the ladder, you can increase your access to more apples (more apples = better return). However, the higher you go up the ladder the more unstable the ladder may become. The higher return is compensation for the added risk.

Figure 3.1: The ladder of risk

Higher return / higher risk

Derivatives
Private equity
Small stocks
Large stocks
Corporate bonds
Government bonds
GICs

Lower return / lower risk

Historical investment vehicle data details past returns. Estimation of the risks can help portfolio managers quantify the expected potential outcomes. A competent portfolio manager will allocate your funds across investment vehicles to match your return objectives.

Expected return and the corresponding risk is a long-term assumption, which over short periods of time, may not occur as expected. During the months or years of outperformance, investors may rationalize recent results and see only returns and not the potential risks. Many times, unusual returns are a result of unexpected events. A good example is the unexpected higher returns in technology and telecom stocks in the run up to Y2K in 1999, and the run up in technology stocks after the COVID-19 pandemic in 2020. History showed that many high-flying technology and telecom stocks suffered significant price declines once normal valuation metrics returned.

COMMON RISKS

Some risks are common to all investors:

- Interest rate risk: The change in a securities value and returns resulting from a change in interest rates.
- Market risk: The variability in portfolio values and returns resulting from fluctuations in the overall market.
- Inflation risk: A factor affecting all securities is purchasing power risk. An example is when your $100 investment earns 1 percent over the year, but the cost of living that year increased by 2.5 percent. Your (now) $101 is not maintaining its purchasing power.
- Business risk: The risk of investing in a particular industry or environment.
- Financial risk: The risk of debt financing or financial leverage.
- Liquidity risk: The risk of a lack of a market to trade an investment (for example, a low number of potential buyers).
- Currency risk: The uncertainty of returns due to fluctuations in investments denominated in foreign currencies.
- Country risk: The political and economic stability that affects the viability of a given country's economy.

SYSTEMATIC OR MARKET RISKS

Systematic risk is the pervasive, far-reaching, and perpetual market risk that reflects a variety of troubling factors. Market crashes are often caused by the unexpected arrival of a risky event, and we don't know how it will end. The resulting uncertainty affects most asset prices and broad markets in a negative way. In the past fifty years alone, major market declines resulted unexpectedly due to:

- 2022   Russia invades Ukraine and unexpected inflation pressures appear
- 2020   COVID-19 pandemic
- 2016   Brexit vote
- 2012   European debt crisis
- 2008   Subprime mortgage crisis
- 2002   War in Iraq
- 2001   9/11 Terrorist attacks
- 2000   Y2K scare and Dot com bubble burst
- 1998   Asian currency crisis
- 1990   Iraq invades Kuwait
- 1987   Black Monday—Dow Jones drops 23% in one day
- 1986   Savings and Loan crisis
- 1981   Inflation hits all time high
- 1974   Arab Oil Embargo / Richard Nixon resigns
- 1973   US military leaves Vietnam

The news may refer to some of the riskier events as "Black Swans" to imply how rare the expected occurrences are.

OTHER RISKS

Other risks are specific to investors' choices. The risks described below do not have the traditional trade-off of higher risk translating into compensating higher return. These are risks that may be non-compensating.

CONCENTRATION RISK

Assume that your portfolio holds twenty-five stocks. You feel comfortable that you are adequately diversified. Then one day you note that the value of your portfolio is down 20 percent in a month. Upon closer inspection, you realize that almost half of the fund's money was invested in technology-related companies. Upon further review, you realize that rising interest rates and recent valuation concerns in technology companies is causing downward pressure on many of these companies' share prices. This is concentration risk. Despite holding many stocks, many of them were exposed to the same risk factors.

ACTIVE MANAGEMENT RISK

Active managers are tasked with the buying and selling of investments. They believe they can pick stocks better than other managers. They think their portfolio will outperform the portfolios of other managers and any benchmark for which their investment strategy is designed. The primary problem is: in an ever-changing market, can active managers achieve persistent outperformance? Research would suggest they can't. Warren Buffett famously wagered one million dollars that an S&P 500 index fund, over the course of a decade, would outperform a basket of hedge funds after costs, fees, and expenses. He comfortably won the bet at the end of 2017.

Active managers are famous for their stories of outperformance. How they outsmarted and outmaneuvered the markets. The problem is that the markets are a highly competitive arena of smart and highly motivated investors, all competing to gain a trading advantage. All this active research and trading translates into a relatively efficient investment market. The only way to beat the market is take more risk, in the right securities, at the right time. Each year, a group of random managers will achieve the goal of outperforming the market. The problem is that investors would need to spot these managers in advance, and hope that when they discover them, their outperformance continues.

> "The problem that people don't understand is that active managers, almost by definition, have to be poorly diversified. Otherwise, they're not really active. They have to make bets. What that means is there's a huge dispersion of outcomes that are totally consistent with just chance. There is no skill involved. It's just good luck or bad luck."
> —Eugene Fama

Seeking a "star active manager" is human nature. Clients are, of course, looking for a good track record in the somewhat irrational hope that it might indicate good future results. We elevate these managers to another level as we assume they can tell us the future. Investors want a special genius that can see the see the world more clearly.

> "The number of managers that can successfully pick stocks are fewer than you'd expect by chance. So, why even play that game? You don't need to."
> —David Booth

Active management is a great marketing approach, just not a very productive approach.

CHASING PAST PERFORMANCE

Any time you read an investment fund prospectus or any investing material, you're going to come across a phrase similar to this: "Past success does not guarantee future performance." Asset management firms are required by securities law to say that past returns of an asset do not imply that the future returns will be the same.

Investors seek out historically good returns. It is human nature to look for past winners. The outperformance may imply an above average manager. The question should be, "Why did the investment, the advisor, or the investment manager perform the way they did?" Was it luck, skill, or an unexpected return of a given sector in the market? Investors and advisors would be better served understanding how markets and asset pricing work to evaluate past returns.

Another problem with judging based on past returns is that you don't capture past returns unless you already own the fund. The expected continued outperformance may not occur, as a manager's future stock selections fail to keep pace in the ever-evolving and highly competitive asset pricing market.

Chasing past performance can lead the unsuspecting investor to misunderstand risk.

VALUATION RISK

Valuation risk is when asset prices become susceptible to high valuations that may not be sustainable. The primary problem occurs when earning growth rates level off or decline.

After many years of spectacular growth in the 1990s, it was assumed or expected that growth rates of earnings for some technology stocks could be 30 percent or more per year. These high expected growth rates pushed technology stocks to all-time highs. The problem occurs when the industry assumes higher earnings growth rates and the stock prices rise for extended periods, investors may forget that valuations matter (and that growth is not eternal).

For example, in the year 2000, two large successful US technology companies, Cisco and Intel, were priced around $82 and $74 per share, respectively. They were the future of technology. Two years later, their prices were $14 and $15, respectively. They were still the future of technology, but their share prices caused significant wealth destruction for shareholders.

In late 1999 and early 2000, Canada experienced extreme valuations in JDS Uniphase, Ballard Power, Nortel, and Celestica. These companies experienced major share price corrections and some of them even went bankrupt.

The demise of the share prices could be partly blamed on "expected growth rate assumptions" that were not achievable. Growth rates are not a linear projection. Competition, changing customer preferences, changes in technology, rising input costs, defecting talent, and management missteps are just a few of the issues that can alter future earnings growth prospects.

Valuation risk is very real and very dangerous. Upward market momentum will always reverse once the high growth companies experience more normalized growth rate and analysts apply more normal valuation metrics. Once momentum changes, the decline in share value can be significant. (Please see "The irony of growth" in Appendix 3.)

SPECULATION RISK

Speculation risk is a more dangerous form of valuation risk and is not always easy to see during a continued rise in investment values. Speculation can be due, in part, to investor herd mentality, fear of missing out (FOMO), and the "greater fool" theory. The greater fool theory is the idea that, during a rising market, one can make money by buying overvalued assets and selling them for future profit, because it will always be possible to find someone who is willing to pay a higher price. An asset value that keeps rising may result in the perception that it is not that risky. Speculators often have great conviction in their expectation of the future. Speculative bubbles rely on attracting more naïve speculators to drive up the price.

Investors are looking for a return. What better investment choice than a speculative asset that appears to just keep going up? Getting a return is as simple as paying $100/share and selling for $160/share. That does not appear complicated or risky, as you made a return of 60 percent. The problem is that your buyer, assuming they want the same percentage return, would need to find a fool to buy it at $256/share. This fool would have to find an even greater fool to sell to, at $410/share, if they seek the same 60 percent return. Once prices stop increasing, the game of easy returns is over—it becomes a game of "hot potato."

A good example is Bitcoin and other cryptocurrencies. A new technology can make many early adopters wealthy. The rising prices in the crypto space can make it appear that high returns and the expectation of future price increases is highly likely. However, it is unclear why holding Bitcoin should have a positive expected return. Bitcoin has no claim on future cash flows as one gets with a stock, bond, or rental asset. Future returns from simply holding bitcoin depend on it appreciating in value versus another asset. This is, by definition, a speculative asset.

Months, or even years, of rising prices make speculative assets appear less risky. However, the investment space is highly speculative and is the subject of extreme price risk. What is the expected future return of unregulated crypto coins or any speculative asset? That is anybody's guess. Just remember the eternal lesson. If something seems too good to be true, it probably is.

NEWS RISK

Just because a story gets a lot of news coverage doesn't necessarily mean it's representative of what's going on in the investing world. This is an issue with news, a business that's incentivized to address its audience's interests and not necessarily its need.

MARKETING RISK

Marketing sells curiosity and can be very persuasive. It makes us feel we are missing out on the better choices of cars, vacations, clothing, food, and investments. Allowing the fear of missing out, referred to as "FOMO," to influence your buy and sell choices, increases the odds that you will make decisions you will later regret. Investors may see advertisements of elements of investing they don't completely understand and feel like they should participate. If you do decide to go against the crowd, there can be lingering thoughts and doubt on whether you made the right decision. Matt Damon, a famous actor, promotes (in a video) an investment idea with the tag line "Fortune favors the brave." Yes, "fortune favors the brave"; that makes sense—you expect higher returns with higher risk. However, promoting cryptocurrency is part fantasy and fakery. Think of it like betting on the long shot at the horse track. There should be a disclaimer with Matt's message: "Fortune does not favor the uninformed."

YOU ARE THE RISK

Our whole lives are about managing risk. We calculate and assess risk relative to benefit (return) all day and every day of our lives. The risk is always there. How are you managing it?

Look both ways before you cross the street

We would expect investors to consider and interpret information differently, resulting in different reactions and decisions. The important part of investor risk is: where did they get their investment idea, what past information influenced the decision, who encouraged the decision, and why did they act on the investment decision?

There are risks, and then there is the ignorance of not understanding risks

Tiger Woods, the famous US golfer, is a good example of not respecting the consequences of one's decisions. Tiger, at the height of his golfing career in the 2000s, reportedly took up training with the Navy Seals. It is reported that the physical stress of the training, which included combat training and jumping out of airplanes, took a toll on his body. This may have resulted in the well-documented decline of his golfing career. In simple terms, Tiger may not have considered the importance of looking both ways before crossing the street. He ignored or was indifferent to the consequences of his actions and how they could affect his day job.

"Investors have a tendency to be their own worst enemy."
—Benjamin Graham

The critical part of investor risk is awareness. If you are aware of and think through the long-term payoffs and probabilities, there is a better chance of managing the risks.

Investments are not the problem. Your investment decisions are!

UNDERSTAND AND MANAGE RISK

"No astronaut launches into space with fingers crossed. That's not how we deal with risk."
—Astronaut, musician, and author Chris Hadfield

Risk and uncertainty are an integral part of life and investing. Your knowledge and experience guide you through risk-management decisions every day. Fear is the risk of something happening—something you don't want to happen. Manage the fear by understanding and respecting risk. Take calculated risks that offer adequate compensation. With investing, the better you and your advisors understand how markets work, the risks of investing, and how you react to risks, the better equipped you are to make informed investment choices.

Investment management is risk management

TAKEAWAYS:
- Investing risk is inseparable from return.
- Risk is the perception of how one feels about the odds of an outcome.
- Perceived risk affects expected returns and asset valuations.
- Understand how you perceive risk and how it affects your investment decision-making.

Chapter 4

Predictions and Expectations

Investors want to know what's going to happen

What stocks to buy or sell? Where are the markets or interest rates going? Which investment managers will do the best? Investors are looking for someone to tell them what is going to happen.

All investment returns are dependent, to varying degrees, on future events

The world is often more complex and harder to understand than people acknowledge. We create stories to rationalize what happened, explain why it happened, what it means, and what will happen next. Predicting creates a loop of expectations, which leads to more assumptions, more rationalizations, and more complications. Investing is a game conducted in a noisy arena. History keeps the score, while participants, spectators, and the media shout out their predictions of the future.

Tell me what you think the market will do next year!

Investors often expect their financial advisors to predict unpredictable outcomes. Worse yet, the advisors will oblige them with a prediction on just about anything. This can increase risk and reduce the odds of a successful outcome.

"Prediction addiction," a phrase coined by Jason Zweig, refers to events that are not predictable, like the direction of the stock market or the future price of a particular stock or mutual fund. Investors crave predictions and want to believe that some guru can tell them the next winning investment. When a prediction comes true, it can create a **"confidence buzz."**

> "The brain highlights what it imagines as patterns; it disregards contradictory information. So limited is our knowledge that we resort, not to science, but to shamans."
> —Benoit Mandelbrot

The investment industry has no shortage of confident-sounding predictions on stock picking, market timing, economics, and hot fund managers. The investment industry is constantly evaluating new information and predicting what is next. Investors have a compulsive desire to have an opinion on, or make sense of, just about everything. Predictions are often based on the investor's intuitive views. Any conflicting views presented are met with a ready-made answer. What gets in the way of rational, clear thinking are those ready-made answers, and investors can't help but have them.

> **"The human desire for predictability and order will result in people sometimes seeing patterns that they believe will deliver certain outcomes. This human desire is often encouraged by promoters who know how to turn dysfunctional thinking into cash—their cash. Unfortunately, our brains can conspire against us when it comes to successful investing. Much of the work a successful investor must do is related to avoiding emotional or psychological mistakes. Even a random number generator will spit out results that a human brain will see as a pattern."**
> —Benoit Mandelbrot

Investors are not competing with themselves. They are competing with all investors, as represented by market averages. In the example in Appendix 1, readers are asked to select one stock each year for ten years. The return over the ten years is the compounded culmination of the ten years. The objective of the game is to pick (or predict) which is the better returning investment each year, relative to the average. The compounded return, with no prediction work, was 8 percent. The question we're trying to answer: does doing all the work predicting and making investment choices each year generate a better return than the average?

Randomly, some predictions will be correct

INVESTORS HAVE EXPECTATIONS

Expectations are part of everyday life. You may experience, at some time, a classic expectation let down while getting your morning coffee. Let us assume you are in line at your favorite drive-through coffee place, and you see four cars in front of you. You estimate that each car will be served in under thirty seconds and assume that you will have your favorite morning beverage in around two minutes. Three minutes go by, and no cars have moved. Six minutes and you have moved one car length. You now have cars behind you, and you are unable to change your mind. Eight minutes have now passed, and you have not ordered yet. You're losing faith and patience, and you're worried something must be wrong. Your expectations have not been met and someone or some technical glitch is to blame.

We buy and sell investments based on expectations

It's human nature to think about and predict the future; investing is no different. Investing is an expectation of the future that we transact today. Investors use all type of investment information, processes, and a whole lot of intuition to set their expectations. Investors' expectations about outcomes will be affected as they interpret new information.

EXAMPLE 4.1: ABC COMPANY

Let's assume you have been researching companies that make wireless fire alarms. One company that you are particularly interested in is called ABC Company.

April: You buy shares in ABC for $10 a share. Your expectation is that the company is doing well, and shares may go to $12 in the next year.

June: Company announces a deal with a big customer and the shares rise to $16 a share. Your expectations were exceeded, and you now feel the shares should go to $20 a share.

August: Company announces a safety defect in one of its best-selling products and shares decline to $13 a share. Your expectations were not met, but you feel the shares will recover to $16 a share.

December: Company has made no material announcements and the shares are trading at $11 a share. You have mixed emotions and expectations, and you are not sure what do to with the shares.

Investing is journey into uncertainty and can be an emotional and financial roller coaster. Despite your expectations, trying to predict what news a company may release, how investors may react to this news, and the future price of a stock are nothing more than educated guesses.

> "He who sees the past as surprise-free is bound to have a future full of surprises."
> —Amos Tversky

NEEDLE IN A HAYSTACK

A needle in a haystack is a great metaphor for the difficulties of finding the next great wealth-creating stock. The goal of investing is to capture future investment returns when and where they may occur. Investors, financial advisors, investment managers, and analysts are all in search of future investment returns to enhance long-term wealth creation.

It is widely known that stock returns have exceeded bond returns, and bond returns have exceeded Treasury Bill returns from 1926 to 2019. However, that does not mean all stocks are created equal. Companies listed on the market must not only compete to serve ever-evolving customer and societal demands but must earn a profit and grow shareholder wealth. Deciding today which companies will fail and which will experience massive success is a tall order.

A November 2020 working paper, "Wealth Creation in the US Public Stock Markets 1926 to 2019" by Hendrick Bessembinder, a business professor at Arizona State University, looks back over nine decades of US financial history. The study examined the shareholder wealth creation of over 26,000 publicly traded companies. Bessembinder defines wealth creation as cash distributions and capital appreciation per firm in excess of the one-month Treasury Bill return.

The report concluded:

- US stock market investments increased shareholder wealth, on net, by $47.4 trillion between 1926 and 2019.
- 42% of publicly listed stocks created shareholder wealth.
- 58% of publicly listed stocks led to reduced shareholder wealth.
- 4%, or approximately 1,000 stocks, accounted for $35 trillion, or 74%, of the wealth creation.
- 0.003% or 86 stocks accounted for 50%, or $24 trillion, of the total shareholder wealth.

The report concludes that a positive skew exists for the big winners that have produced large gains versus the majority of stocks, which have produced losses or mediocre returns. The research indicates that the outperformance of the stock market is largely attributable to outstanding returns generated by a relatively few stocks.

To benefit from the biggest wealth creators, investors would have had to make the investment before it became a big winner and hold onto it during its ascent to the top. Recent examples of the wealth creators are Apple, Amazon, and Walmart.

To find the future winners, the equivalent of finding needles in a haystack, investors have three basic choices:

1) Research and select the next best eighty-five stocks in advance. This will require having lottery-winning-type luck. Selecting only a few individual stocks exposes the investor to both huge potential gains and disappointing losses.
2) Buy the current best eighty-five stocks and assume their future distributions and price appreciations will continue indefinitely. This approach can expose investors, not only to the next General Electric, but also the next WorldCom and Enron.
3) Buy a broad market of stocks using an index or asset class fund. The fund should include a broad range of large and small companies, including the most recent

winners. Hold on to the index or asset class fund and slowly build wealth by collecting the return premiums (market, value, small cap, and profitability), and allowing the portfolio to compound over the long term.

The irony of this research study is that some money managers may have assumed they could research and select the next best eighty-five stocks in advance. Two prominent money managers to watch—both have chosen the "go find the next best winners" approach—are Cathie Woods of Ark Investment Management Company and Chase Coleman of Tiger Global Management.

Remember, the goal of investing is to capture returns and manage risk. Most readers of *7 Steps*, will find more comfort and logic in investing in a broad market using an index or asset class fund. This approach will, by its very nature, hold all the current winners and likely most of the future ones as well.

CAN YOU PREDICT THE FUTURE?

> "I got this wrong."
> —Shopify CEO announces plan to lay off 10 percent of the staff. July 26, 2022

Expectations are utilized by buyers and sellers, and all this information is reflected in the current price of a stock. The best way to beat the market is to make better predictions of the future. Many investors believe they can identify "mispriced" securities and convert that knowledge to higher returns. Unless you are a descendant of Nostradamus, how could you have predicted with any certainty the news, the reaction, and the change in price of ABC shares as discussed in example 4.1?

> "Don't believe everything you think."
> —Robert Fulghum

There are eight billion people on the planet. About five billion of them are considered middle class. The middle class is an ambiguous social classification, broadly reflecting the ability to lead a comfortable life. The middle class usually enjoy stable housing, healthcare, and educational opportunities (including college) for their children, reasonable retirement, and job security. The growing global middle class has an enormous impact on consumption and savings rates.

There are tens of thousands of companies competing to serve ever-changing consumer preferences. These companies constantly evolve and innovate to meet consumer and societal demands, while seeking to earn a profit and grow shareholder wealth.

Imagine you see a lone forecaster on a media platform forecasting the future of a stock or market. Can they really predict and profit from the future of a stock, a group of stocks, or the markets better than other investors—with consistent accuracy? If there was such a wizard, one who could time markets and pick winning stocks better than the market, this would be akin to finding Bigfoot or the Loch Ness monster, and there would be statistical evidence that they exist. There are random winners, but there is no record of a persistently successful stock picker or market timer in over one hundred years of market data.

Can you teach prediction?

If you take golf lessons, you may become a better golfer. If you take investing lessons, you may make fewer investing mistakes, but it doesn't imply that you will be better at forecasting the future.

> "People don't know the boundaries of their expertise; we live in a subjective world and can't separate what we can forecast from what we can't."
> —Daniel Kahneman

Investors misunderstand skill or acquired skill about predicting the future. The study of finance will give you a better understanding of past, current, and expected returns and risks. It's unlikely that more training in finance will give you the skill to predict the future of unexpected outcomes that affect returns and risks.

Random walk theory

A random walk is one in which future steps or directions cannot be predicted on the basis of past history. Therefore, it assumes the past movement or trend of a stock price or market cannot be used to predict its future movement. In short, random walk theory proclaims that stocks take a random and unpredictable path that makes all methods of predicting stock prices futile in the long run.

Predict less plan more

Predictions are just that—predictions. One may randomly predict an outcome, but there is no evidence that one has consistently predicted the future. If there was someone that could predict the future better than the masses, we would have evidence of this. They would be the greatest investor of all time.

STOCKS ARE PRICED ON EXPECTATIONS

On April 19, 2022, after the markets closed, Netflix released their first quarter financial information and provided their expectations for the next quarter. The price on the close of April 19, 2022, was $348.61 US per share.

The report stated the following quarterly numbers:

- Earnings per share (EPS) of $3.53 versus the expected $2.89
- Revenue was $7.87 billion versus the expected $7.93 billion

Based on these numbers, you may expect the stock price to go up. However, the company disclosed that they lost 200,000 subscribers when they had expected to gain 2.5 million net new subscribers during the first quarter. Analysts were reported to have predicted that number would be closer to 2.7 million. During the same period a year ago, Netflix added 3.98 million net new paid subscribers. The company cited growing competition from recent streaming launches by traditional entertainment companies. Netflix estimated they could lose another two million net subscribers in quarter two of 2022.

The stock price at the close of the next day, April 20, 2022, was $226.19, a decline of $122.42 per share, or **-35.12** percent. Shareholder expectations of continued growth were crushed, and the new share price reflected the new expectations.

FAANG STOCKS—EXPECTED AND UNEXPECTED

The so-called FAANG stocks—Facebook (now Meta), Amazon, Apple, Netflix, and Google (now Alphabet)—are a good example of unexpected outcomes. Over the ten years from September 2010 to August 2020, a portfolio of the five stocks, held in proportion to their market capital weights, would have delivered an average return of 34.25 percent per year. I doubt investors in September 2020 had expected those returns.

So, what explains the FAANG's high realized returns? The unexpected happened! Sales and earnings growth turned out much higher than expected over this decade. If investors had expected the 34.25 percent returns over the past decade, the prices of these five stocks would have been significantly higher in September 2010. In other words, the high expected returns would have been priced into the stock back in 2010.

Given the great returns over the past ten years, what can be expected for the annualized return over the next decade? Can the high expected growth rates continue?

As of the end of September 2022, four of the five stocks lagged the broad US market, with Amazon, Meta, and Netflix suffering big-time losses. The reversal in price is a reminder that investors should be cautious when assuming past returns will continue in the future.

"Expected" and "unexpected" describe the very nature of the uncertainty of investing. Asset values are based on assumptions that change with new information. Everything we assume about the future is priced in today. The new information, which arrives randomly, will prove or disprove our assumptions.

Trying to guess which specific stocks will experience unexpected, good news and which may experience unexpected bad news, and how investors will react, is too difficult, and leaves too much to chance. Long-term pension-style investing is about the odds, and reliable and consistent returns. It's possible you can guess the unexpected—it's just not probable.

JIM CRAMER OVERCOME WITH EMOTION AS HE APOLOGIZES FOR BEING WRONG ABOUT META

On October 27, 2022, Jim Cramer was on CNBC. He became overcome with emotion as he apologized for being wrong about Facebook's parent company, Meta. Meta shares closed trading at $97.94 that day.

Jim is a legend on Wall Street and an investment media icon. Through his personal connections and his highly successful investment show, he has unparalleled access to company CEOs, investment managers, financial analysts, and other financial journalists. Mark Zuckerberg, CEO of Meta Platforms, appeared on CNBC's "Mad Money with Jim Cramer" on June 22, 2022. Jim, as the optimistic personality he is, was very positive about why investors should consider investing in Meta shares. At that time, Meta shares (FB) were trading at around $170, down from their high of $378 in September of 2021.

On October 27, 2022, it was a different story. Jim, in his discussion with co-host David Faber, said, "I made a mistake here. I was wrong. I trusted this management team. That was ill-advised. The hubris here is extraordinary and I apologize."

When told he wasn't the only person to think Meta's stock would perform well, Cramer replied, "I don't really care about that. I screwed up."

The Facebook story is not a criticism of Jim Cramer. The point is to highlight how difficult it is to predict future information and how the market participants may react to that information. Providing a prediction is easy, profiting from the prediction is not.

CAPTURE MARKETS WITH A RULES-BASED SYSTEMATIC PROCESS AND STRUCTURE RATHER THAN PREDICTIONS

Markets are an ever-evolving pricing mechanism that reflects the expectations of economic growth, innovation, societal demands, and consumer preferences. Understand, respect, and appreciate how markets work and how to use markets to your advantage. There is a big difference between predicting a market move or next week's winning stocks and a rules-based, systematic portfolio process and structure focused on capturing market returns. A prediction approach may be exciting and fun but is fundamentally flawed as a long-term investment strategy to capture return and manage risk.

Markets have been the greatest creator of mass wealth in history

The markets represent the growth of capitalism at work in the economy. Historically, they have provided a long-term return that has offset inflation. (Please see randomness of asset class returns in Appendix 5.) Rather than view the market universe in terms of individual stocks, investors should view markets in the broader sense of the equity premium, value premium, small cap premium, and profitability premium. These are discussed in the coming chapters and appendices. *7 Steps* is about a portfolio process and structure designed to improve the odds of capturing these premiums, while managing the risk of the overall portfolio.

TAKEAWAYS:

- Stocks are priced based on investors' predictions or expectations of the future.

- Research indicates the statistical difficulty in predicting the few significant winners in a large sample size.

- The unexpected will have the most significant impact on positive and negative returns.

- Randomly, some predictions will be correct.

Chapter 5

Strategy and Execution

As in the dieting culture, there is no shortage of investment ideas

Everyone wants a great investment experience over their lifetime, but many don't understand what it takes to make this happen. Often, we think investing is primarily about short-term return. Return is what we seek. Return makes us feel good emotionally and financially. Long-term investment strategies and risk management seem secondary. Investment strategy seems like homework and risk management lacks any joy at all.

In every aspect of life, including health and investing, your openness to evidence-based information, in combination with reflection, planning, strategy, and consistent execution, will have an impact on the odds of accomplishing your goals.

> "If you fail to plan, you are planning to fail."
> —Benjamin Franklin

STRATEGY DRIVES THE PLAN TOWARDS THE OBJECTIVE; EXECUTION IMPROVES THE ODDS OF ACCOMPLISHING THE OBJECTIVE.

The success of a strategy will primarily be driven by how one defines the objective, charts the direction, develops effective strategic moves, and pursues what needs to be done. The better conceived the strategy and the more competently it is executed, the higher the odds of long-term success.

Capture return and manage risk

Identifying the objectives is straightforward and can be as simple as "I want a better portfolio experience." The experience may mean better returns, less investment anxiety, or more confidence in the investment approach. We can all relate to the objective, "I want to lose weight and get into better shape." The identification of the objective is a great start. The difficult part is developing a strategy that can be easily executed, over months and years, to improve the odds of achieving the objective. This may explain why health and fitness has become a trillion-dollar industry, and there are endless investment advertisements in the media.

Investment strategies may be based on three different approaches:

1) Intuitive, opinion-based approach
   An intuitive approach is more emotional, instinctive, and creative.

2) Rules-based, systematic approach
   A rules-based approach is more evidence based, methodical, and consistent.

3) Some combination of 1 and 2

In any given endeavor such as sports, business, diet, and much of life, a rules-based, systematic approach will improve the odds of attaining the given objective. A rules-based technique uses evidence-based data to create a formulaic approach. This reduces the impact of investment and market noise on judgment. A systematic approach will increase consistency in execution.

> "Any sound long-range investment program requires patience and perseverance. Perhaps that is why so few investors follow any plan. Investment success is the purpose of investment planning; but a by-product of a good plan is piece of mind."
> —Sir John Templeton

A good plan only works if the participants have logical tools in place to manage their emotional impulses. Like rules in a game that keep players in check, a strategy needs tools to increase self-control. Investors tend to procrastinate fixing their portfolios, and their lack of self-control can lead them to make misguided investment decisions.

A strategy for health and well-being

I created my own rules-based approach to improving my physical and mental health because I get easily stressed and enjoy food more than exercise. Stress is stressful, food is pleasure, and exercise is work. I had to figure out a simple, yet intelligent and executable plan to deal with this. I decided on the following process and structure that is easy to maintain and consistently executable:

Food: I don't eat French fries or potato chips and have significantly reduced consumption of salt, processed sugar, processed meat, and flour. I eat more protein-based plant food, and I am more selective in choices of meat-based protein. I can eat the odd *sin* food, but in reduced amounts and frequency. I don't keep any "sin" foods at home or at the office. If I'm hungry, I drink water and eat unsalted almonds.

Exercise: I keep an Excel spreadsheet that documents all the units of exercise I do per day, over a given month. I get points for doing stairs in my office building, lifting weights, doing sit-ups, running, yard work, long walks, hiking, and so on. The key to the spreadsheet is to document daily physical and aerobic exercise for both muscle and heart health.

Mental health: I make a point of saying "have a nice day" at least five times a day. I try and lose myself listening to three to five great songs (with my earbuds) while relaxing or reflecting the good things from the past, present, or future. I only read news from reputable publishing sources. I only use Instagram to watch comedy.

Intermittent fasting: Two or four times a week I will have my last meal around two or three p.m. and will not eat again until eleven a.m. the following day. It's easy to miss a dinner and skip the evening snacks.

Accountability: I weigh myself once a week, on Friday mornings, by taking a picture of the scale with my phone. There are weeks, unfortunately, that I gain weight. But this is a twenty-year endeavor, and I remind myself that what matters is the process (managing food intake) and structure (consistent physical exercise and mental relaxation). I don't look back; I look forward.

It's 10% having a great plan (diet and exercise) and 90% implementation and consistent execution of the plan that makes it work.

This simple, executable strategy increases the odds that I can keep my weight down and maintain my strength and mental well-being. Only I can complicate my simple process and structure. Long-term successful investing, as set out in the *7 Steps,* has many similarities with creating a process and structure-driven healthy lifestyle.

> "85% of feeling better is linked to lifestyle changes"
> —Phil Stutz

LIFE CYCLE

Life cycle refers to a series of stages you will pass through during your lifetime. Different stages involve unique needs, cash flows, obligations, and perceptions of risks and returns. The life cycle stage will affect your objectives, preferences, and constraints. This, in turn, affects how you will design and implement your investment strategies.

The young investor stage, age 20 to 39: This is the time to build human capital, also referred to as earnings potential, by getting an education and acquiring more skills. This group should start to build their investment capital by setting up a systematic monthly savings plan. Even though this group has decades of earnings ahead of them, it is critical at this stage to develop good habits around saving and consumption. Although their assets are just starting to accumulate, they should seek advice on wills, estate issues, and life insurance. In addition to saving and investing in an RRSP to reduce taxes, the best forced saving plan is to buy a place to live. Mortgage payments can be a great forced savings plan.

The accumulator stage, age 40 to 59: This group usually has a stable career and a better idea of where they are and where they would like their life to go. This group is assumed to have matured physically, psychologically, and financially. At this stage, they have likely lived through an economic recession or market downturn in the capital markets, and possibly a major event like a job loss or divorce. Their incomes are likely higher and more stable than for those in the young investor stage. They still feel young, but they understand that retirement is on the horizon. Their views around risks are changing, and they may be looking for a balance of growth, stability, and security in their investment process.

The transitional retiree, age 60 to 70: This stage begins with preretirement years, which coincide with the highest and most stable salary in their careers. Household expenses are stabilized, children are self-sufficient or beginning to be self-sufficient, and savings rates are at their highest. This stage evolves into ending their career and transitioning into full retirement. This group may do some selective spending on leisure, toys, and home renovations. Most are healthy at this stage, and they need a plan for a long retirement. They may be looking for balance of moderate growth to maintain purchasing power and reduced portfolio volatility.

The retiree, age 71 to 78: In this stage, the investor will have moved into full retirement. Faced with the fact their productive earning years are in the past, they are adjusting to living within their financial means, utilizing draws from their pensions and investment assets. They are adjusting to a slower-paced life, with increased attention to staying healthy. At this stage, their portfolios need to be properly allocated and highly diversified to reduce and manage risk. The 64,000-dollar question for this group (from the CBS game show in the 1950s) is, how much should, or could, one withdraw from their investments and still have enough if they live to one hundred?

The mature retiree, age 79 and beyond: People in this group are now living a quieter life; they are living on the pure distribution of their savings and pensions. Their rhythm of life and spending is determined by the state of their health. At this stage, distributions to the children need to be balanced with their own life expectancy and potential increases in the costs of living. As in the previous stage, risk needs to be managed through a properly allocated and highly diversified portfolio, with an emphasis on lower-risk asset classes. At this stage, part of their investment assets may be considered intergenerational, meaning that there is a plan for wealth transfer to family, and it is managed accordingly. Their estate wishes must be clearly documented in a will to ensure that their estate passes smoothly to their chosen beneficiaries.

INVESTOR RISK TOLERANCE

Decisions made during the investment life cycle will be affected by the investor's tolerance for risk. Defining risk tolerance, like defining risk, can be subjective and complicated. It is not just risk that matters, but your perceptions of risk and how it may change depending on circumstances. Individual investors often refer to risk as "losing money." Institutional investors, on the other hand, refer to risk as "portfolio volatility."

Investor risk tolerance can be better understood when we look at it as a reflection of our willingness, ability, and need to put our savings at risk as we seek returns.

The willingness to take on risk may depend on:

- The investor's mental and emotional ability to handle uncertainty
- The psychological acceptance of a decline in portfolio value
- The psychological acceptance of a permanent loss of wealth

Willingness to take on risk can be subjective and can change as the perception of risk changes.

The ability or capacity to take on risk may depend on:

- Stage of life and time horizon
- Level of wealth and value of funds invested, relative to other sources of income or assets
- Family situation
- Tax situation
- Liquidity

Ability or capacity is more objective and based on the investor's specific situations.

The need to take on risk may depend on:

- Need for capital gains over income
- Need to save for retirement
- Need to diversify from the other investments (i.e., a private business or commercial real estate)

EXAMPLE 5.1: TWO INVESTORS AND RISK TOLERANCE

Jayden is forty years old, in a well-paying career, and he is saving for retirement. He lost money during the past two years in his RRSP because of a market correction in cannabis-related investments. He does not want to see his savings decline, so he is choosing low-risk term deposits.

Jayden has the ability (based on his stage of life) and the need (building for retirement) but not the willingness to tolerate more risk.

Gabriela is seventy-five years old, retired, and on a pension, and she is drawing down her savings to fund her living expenses. She wants to invest a large part of her savings into electric vehicles companies.

Gabriela has the willingness to seek opportunity returns but not the ability to tolerate potential loss, or the need to accept more risk.

Suitability

Suitability is another risk-tolerance consideration. Before making a recommendation, financial advisors have a duty to take steps that ensure the investment is suitable for the investor's goals, needs, and risk tolerance. The suitability assessment includes a requirement that advisors must know and understand the characteristics and risks associated with any investment product approved or recommended to clients.

THE INVESTMENT POLICY STATEMENT

The investment strategy starts with documenting all of your investment objectives, constraints, and preferences. These are combined in what is often referred to as the Investment Policy Statement. A typical Investment Policy Statement may include:

1) **Client description:**
   Age, income, education, employment, investment experience

2) **Investor objectives:**
   a. Return objective:
   b. Risk tolerance (range of portfolio investments)
       Low risk   _____ %
       Moderate risk   _____ %
       High risk   _____ %
       Speculative risk _____ %
       Total   _____ %

   Risk tolerance, as explained in chapter 3, is based on the investor's willingness, ability, and need to tolerate risk.

3) **Constraints and preferences:**
   a. Liquidity needs
       Need for cash and cash flow over time to cover expenditures

   b. Time horizon
       When the investments are expected to be invested

   c. Laws and regulations
       Tax and CRA restrictions

   d. Taxes
       Minimize income, capital gain, or dividend income

   e. Unique preferences and circumstances
       Any restriction you may want to apply to the portfolio

THREE PORTFOLIO APPROACHES

The choice of portfolio approach will reflect your investment style, personal views, and understanding of how markets work. The objective is to use the portfolio approach that provides the better odds of long-term investment success.

A portfolio is just a collection of investments or building blocks that add up to 100 percent. The goal is to put the right investment blocks (diversification), in the right proportion (allocation), at the right times, over the lifetime of the portfolio. Setting the asset allocation and selection of investment vehicles is the responsibility of the advisors overseeing the portfolio.

In the formation of a portfolio, investors have a choice of active, passive, or semi-passive investment management. Three common portfolio approaches that incorporate these investment management choices are:

1) **Portfolio of individual stocks (active investment management)**
2) **Portfolio of active mutual funds or managers (active investment management)**
3) **Portfolio of index and asset class funds (passive and semi-passive investment management**

We will examine the three portfolio approaches in chapter 8. We will evaluate the three portfolio approaches relative to the 7 Steps in an evaluation rubric in chapter 10.

There are significant risk and reward trade-offs when choosing any of the three portfolio approaches. These will be discussed in subsequent chapters.

7 STEPS TO A BETTER PORTFOLIO

Think of each of the 7 Steps as a task that needs to be accomplished. The goal is to build and manage a portfolio that is designed to accomplish each Step. Separately, each Step is important to the creation of a portfolio. Combined, they create an efficient and effective portfolio. The 7 Steps to a better portfolio:

1) **Allocate across global capital markets**
2) **Diversify broadly within each market**
3) **Focus on higher expected returns**
4) **Utilize financial science**
5) **Manage strategy risk**
6) **Manage investment choice risk**
7) **Manage costs and taxes**

The *7 Steps* process is not looking to find the perfect portfolio. Perfection is a historical reference, and we are investing in the future. *7 Steps* is just a guide to help you evaluate portfolio choices, processes, and structures in a manner designed to improve the odds of a successful outcome in the long-term.

Each of the 7 Steps is something each investor controls. It is very important that investors make the distinction between what they control and what they don't control. Investors do not control markets, stock prices, interest rates, central banks, corporate earnings, or market sentiment, to name a few. Investors, however, do control each of the 7 Steps.

A detailed explanation of each of the steps can be found in chapter 9. The Steps are then discussed further, relative to three portfolio approaches, in chapter 10.

EXECUTION OF THE STRATEGY

The hardest thing about strategy is not the planning phase, but the execution phase. Even with a great plan, the strategy only works if the right steps are consistently executed over days, months, years, and decades.

Strategy without execution is just a good idea

Executing a plan is like yard work. There is always something else to do other than working in the yard. Procrastination affects execution, which affects the probability of success. The key is to convert the strategy into steps that turn your plans into reality. Completing each task is about taking the time to do it.

MAINTAINING THE STRATEGY

Utilize an intelligent strategy, execute on the strategy, and maintain the strategy in up and down markets.

> "Everyone has a plan until they get punched in the face."
> —Mike Tyson

Markets are volatile. New information can shift investors' emotions from positive to negative and back again. Up markets can result in a false sense of security and cause one to chase the winners. Down markets can affect confidence and cause one to run away from risk. Maintaining a strategy works best when the plan focuses on what you control, to best manage what you don't.

Patience is not inactivity, it's part of the plan

GOOD HABITS

A good investment strategy requires the consistent application of intelligent, yet simple to accomplish, actions that you control. The consistent application of good habits can improve the odds of a long-term, successful outcome in many facets of your life.

Investors may intend to invest in a rational manner. However, their behavior is often impacted by the environment of external impulsions. Investing, like a lifelong commitment to losing weight and getting in better shape, requires a long-term change in behavior. Routine behaviors, repeated overtime become habits.

> "Real change requires you to change behavior – not just your attitude"
> —Phil Stutz

A good sleep, healthy diet, regular exercise, plenty of water, and hand-washing

In the best-selling book, *The Power of Habit*, award-winning *New York Times* business reporter Charles Duhigg explains why habits exist and how they can be changed to improve outcomes. The author points out that habits are the choices we deliberately make at one time, but then stop thinking about, and continue repeating. Developing good habits relating to physical and mental health are critical to increasing the odds of a long-term successful outcome. Developing and maintaining good investing habits consistent with a great investment strategy is critical to improving long-term investment odds.

> "This process within our brains is a three-step loop. First, there is a cue, a trigger that tells your brain to go into automatic mode and which habit to use. Then there is the routine, which can be physical or mental or emotional. Finally, there is a reward, which helps your brain figure out if this particular loop is worth remembering for the future: THE HABIT LOOP."
> —Charles Duhigg

GOOD ADVICE

A portfolio is the creation of an advisor and/or the client. A portfolio is just like a team of investments that are placed together to achieve an objective. A financial advisor is like the coach or general manager of the team investments. The advisor is expected to develop, execute, and maintain a portfolio strategy using their selected investments. The portfolio objective is to capture returns, manage risks, and increase their odds of long-term investment success.

Good advice directs you to trust evidence-based information to make better, more informed decisions to improve the odds of successful outcome.

> "Good financial advisors are good financial physicians. Good advisors possess the knowledge of finance, as good physicians possess knowledge of medicine, and good advisors add to it the skills of good physicians: asking, listening, empathizing, educating, and prescribing."
> —Meir Statman

DON'T MEASURE A STRATEGY BY ITS SUCCESS; MEASURE A STRATEGY BY ITS SUBSTANCE.

Winning a lottery, making a big win in a speculative stock, successfully jumping your bike over a ditch—these are all random acts of success that, if attempted many times, may suffer the mathematical odds of failure. Random outcomes defy odds, get a lot of attention, and may have interesting stories attached to them. They are just random events of good or bad luck.

Luck: Success or failure, apparently brought by chance rather than through one's own actions.

Strategy: A plan of action or policy, designed to achieve a major goal or objective.

A random success or failure should not define a strategy. There is an element of good and bad luck in everyday life. Your job is to manage the bad and capture the good.

We want to believe it will work out, but hope is not a strategy—math-based process and structure is a strategy

Successful long-term investment is founded on an approach based on substance. A rules-based and executable strategy (process) can be carried out with consistency and accountability (structure). This will help you navigate your portfolio decisions through volatile capital markets and improve the odds of a long-term successful outcome.

Investing, like life, is about finding meaning and substance in the choices you make

Strategies, like people, should be measured by substance. There is a relationship between success and surrounding oneself with the right people, using evidence-based research, following a process and structure, being accountable, consistently applying good habits, and having a good moral compass.

TAKEAWAYS:

- Develop an intelligent strategy, execute on the strategy, and maintain the strategy.
- Focus on capturing return and managing risk.
- Good habits add up to better outcomes over time.
- Measure strategy by its substance.

Chapter 6

Markets

The markets are an arena of conflicting opinion!

The market brings together a buyer and a seller. The two of them, by the nature of the transaction, have a different expectation of the future of the investment being transacted. The buyer thinks the investment is attractive and will compensate them with a return. The seller thinks the investment is less attractive, and their savings are better invested elsewhere. They are voting or transacting their expectation or belief for the future, as it relates to a specific asset.

> "One of the funny things about the stock market is that every time one person buys, another sells, and both think they are astute."
> —William Feather

Is now the time to buy shares in Air Canada?

In March 2022, as I write this, it appears the worst of COVID-19 is behind us. A friend remarks that it's obvious that the demand for air travel will rise as global travel restrictions ease. This is a classic example of asset pricing and expectations. Are Air Canada shares a good buy at the current price, or have the expectations of more travel already been priced into the current shares? Will the shares be much higher in one or three years? To buy the shares at the current price, the buyer needs a seller. Can the seller not see the obvious, that the shares are an attractive buy?

How do we know which stocks are going to go up and which stocks are going down in price?

MARKETS

Stocks markets are a venue where buyers and sellers meet to exchange shares in publicly traded companies. Companies become public by selling shares for the first time through the process of an initial public offering (IPO). This activity, with the help of an investment underwriter, helps companies raise necessary capital from investors. This market is commonly referred to as the primary market.

The secondary market, referred to as the stock market, is the market that enables numerous buyers and sellers of securities to meet, interact, and transact. Think of the stock market as a large information processing machine that takes in all the information about a company. All this information affects the transaction price that buyers and sellers agree on. This doesn't mean that a price is always correct; that is a matter of interpretation. However, investors can accept the market price as the best estimated value.

Markets are vital components of a free-market economy because they enable democratized access to trading and the exchange of capital for all investors. Stock markets provide a secure and regulated environment in which market participants can transact in shares and other eligible financial instruments with confidence, and zero to low operational risk. The marketplace is made up of a variety of participants, including market makers, investors, traders, and speculators. These participants operate in the stock market with different roles and functions. For instance, an investor may buy stocks and hold them for the long term, spanning many years, while a trader may enter and exit a position within seconds. A market maker provides necessary liquidity in the market, while someone may trade in derivatives to mitigate the risks involved in other investments.

MARKETS ARE A CENTRAL INSTITUTION OF CAPITALISM

The market is a central institution of capitalism. A company's ability to raise capital (from new investors) is a critical component of its economic expansion. The profits and cash flow a company generates feed back into the business or into the hands of shareholders. Markets allow all of us to participate in human ingenuity, and earn a return for doing so. The profitability of the business will depend on the competency of the company to innovate and satisfy changing consumer demand. Owned by shareholders, companies are regulated by implicit societal pressures and government laws. The market price of a stock reflects the success or failure of a company to meet the expectations of shareholders, stakeholders, and consumers.

MARKETS FACILITATE PRICE DISCOVERY

Price discovery has investors examining tangible and intangible factors, including fundamental and technical research, risk attitudes, and the overall economic and market environment. Price discovery is where the buyer—that is, the demand—agrees on a price with the seller—that is, the supply. Simply put, it is where a buyer and a seller agree on a price and a transaction occurs.

Investing, like life, is full of strong opinions, but one can only transact when the price someone is willing to pay for an asset matches the price someone is willing to sell it for. This is true when buying or selling something on Facebook Marketplace or the Toronto Stock Exchange. For example, someone might say, I only want to pay $10, and a seller says they will only sell at $80. They can put on protest marches, write in blogs, and complain all they want. Other buyers and sellers meet, exchange views, and agree on a price to buy and sell for $40, and get on with it. If either side felt the price was not meeting his or her expected return needs, they would not complete the transaction.

Markets are always reacting to new information in real time

Price discovery is very important because it establishes return and risk expectations. When a price is rising, investor buying may be triggered by the expectation that risks are declining, and future cash flow and earnings growth may be rising. When a price is falling, investor selling may be triggered by the expectation that risks are rising, and that cash flow and future earnings growth may be declining.

TWO STEPS FORWARD, ONE STEP BACK

Markets are an ever-evolving asset pricing mechanism affected by participants' views of new information. The new information and how it is perceived and transacted by buyers and sellers may cause stocks and the markets to increase or decrease. Markets represent companies that innovate, meet changing consumer and societal demands, and grow shareholder wealth. The odds, in a growing and evolving global economy, favor a rising market over time.

Up and down months of the S&P 500 market between 1926 and August 2022:

- For 1160 total months, the average return was 0.96% per month.
- For 727 months in the period (62.7% of the total), the market had positive returns.
- For 430 months in the period (37.1% of the total), the market had negative returns.
- For three months in the period (0.2% of the total), the market had zero returns.

If it feels like investing is two steps forward and one step back, it is.

MARKETS ARE RELATIVELY EFFICIENT

The stock market is an effective and efficient information processing system that reflects the views of millions of buyers and sellers. The market participants have access to all public information, estimates, and perceptions of risk at any given time. Buyers and sellers evaluate available information and interpret this as either a buy, sell, or ignore signal. The buyers' demand and the sellers' supply will meet at a transaction price.

The term "efficient market hypothesis" essentially means that share prices fully reflect all available information.

The hypothesis states:

- Current prices incorporate all available information and expectations.
- Current prices are the best approximation of intrinsic value.
- Price changes are due to new information resulting in a change in perception of value.
- "Mispricing" can occur, but not in predictable patterns that can lead to consistent outperformance.

Ken French, finance professor at Dartmouth College, was once asked, "How efficient are the markets?" He is quoted as saying, **"I'm not sure there is standard metric, so I'll say it's about 87.32 percent."**

EXAMPLE 6.1: THE EFFICIENT MARKET THEORY AND ONE STOCK

On Monday, after the market closed, you find yourself thinking about investing in shares of a company we will refer to as Company #12. Company #12 closed that day at $50/share. The closing price, the last agreed upon price, reflects a price based on buyers and sellers' views of current expectations.

On Tuesday, new information, which may relate to the stock, the economy, interest rates, or a specific industry, will be disseminated by investors. New information may affect how buyers and sellers perceive expected risks and returns of Company #12. On Tuesday, the information is translated into a more positive view of Company #12 and the share price increases by 6%, to a closing price of $53.

Investors are buying and selling shares of Company #12 based on how new information affects their predictions and assumptions. On Wednesday, new information, which may relate to the stock, the economy, interest rates, or a specific industry, will be disseminated by investors. The information and the perception of the information by the buyers and sellers causes the share price to decline by 3.8%, to a closing price of $51.

Investors react to news; news is new information

New information is by definition, new news; that is, news that was not known before. Some investors will do in-depth financial research; some will make decisions based on trading patterns; others may be persuaded by blogs, newsletters, or tea leaves. The collective transaction wisdom of all the buyers and sellers trying to predict the future of Company #12 will set the price. The price will efficiently reflect, at any given time, all available information and expectations of the buyers and sellers.

The problem investors face when predicting the future direction of the stocks is two-fold:

1) Can they predict the new information?
2) Can they predict how other buyers and sellers will react to the new information?

An efficient market implies that share prices reflect investors perception of all publicly available information.

EXAMPLE 6.2: THE EFFICIENT MARKET THEORY AND AN ACTIVE MANAGER

Assume it is Monday morning, March 15, and there is a market with 100 different companies or stocks, labelled #1 to #100. Now imagine there are thirty portfolio managers labeled M1 to M30. Assume each manager will hold 20 of the 100 stocks. For example, assume manager M5 owned stocks 1 to 5, 25 to 29, and 50 to 59 for a total of twenty stock positions. Assume manager M17 owned twenty different stocks. Assume manager M22 owned some of the stocks owned by M5 and M17.

Each stock will change in value, depending on how new news or information affects the perceptions of the buyers or sellers. Portfolio managers face the same problems as individual stock selectors:

1) Can they predict the new information?
2) Can they predict how other buyers and sellers will react to the new information?

How does a manager know which stock will go up and which stock will go down? With managers competing to buy and sell stocks, they, in effect, create the market. If, for some reason, a majority of the thirty money managers thought that new information meant the current share price of Company #7 was attractive and wanted to buy more shares, they would need sellers to sell them the shares. The collective purchases may drive up the price—possibly to a point where current investors find the stock less attractive to own, and as a result, sell their shares. For example, assume Company #7 shares traded at $18 at the market close on Monday. On Tuesday, new news that was perceived to be good resulted in more managers seeking to buy more shares in Company #7, versus managers seeking to sell. The share price of Company #7 gets bid up to $25. This price may create an equilibrium where the buyers can find sellers and agree on a price to transact.

Managers face the same efficient market problem as individual investors. If individual investors were to hire one of the above managers, how would they know which manager in the next year would outperform their peers and possibly outperform the market as well?

What if we don't try to out-predict the market, but rather use how the market works to our advantage?

The efficient market theory suggests that predicting which stocks and which managers will outperform can be difficult without a fully functioning crystal ball. Decades of academic research shows that it is very difficult to outguess market prices, and the odds are stacked against those who try. This is consistent with the idea that information about expected returns is quickly reflected in market prices, allowing investors to rely on those prices to identify differences in expected returns. In chapter 7 and appendices 2, 3, and 4 we will examine how we can use the information in market prices to understand the drivers of expected returns.

THE SAMPLE STOCK MARKET

The sample stock market is my hypothetical stock market that contains 500 publicly traded companies. It is referred to as a "stock market" because the companies are represented by common shares or common stocks. Companies list on a market to raise capital—that is, to issue more shares—and to enable investors to buy and sell its existing shares.

The objective of any investor selecting a publicly traded stock is to capture return and manage risk. This objective is critical to remember as we examine various investment approaches to achieve this goal.

The market is a regulated environment designed to enable buyers and sellers to meet and agree on a price at which to transact. The market is just a venue and has no emotion. Any changes in share prices reflect the buyers' and sellers' perceptions of new information. Positive news may encourage more buyers than sellers, and the increase in demand may drive the share price up. Negative news may discourage buyers and increase the number of sellers, and the price may decline.

Figure 6.1: The sample stock market

Decile																									
1	A	1	2	3	4	5	6	7	8	9	10	11	12	13	14	15	16	17	18	19	20	21	22	23	24	25
2	B	1	2	3	4	5	6	7	8	9	10	11	12	13	14	15	16	17	18	19	20	21	22	23	24	25
2	C	1	2	3	4	5	6	7	8	9	10	11	12	13	14	15	16	17	18	19	20	21	22	23	24	25
3	D	1	2	3	4	5	6	7	8	9	10	11	12	13	14	15	16	17	18	19	20	21	22	23	24	25
3	E	1	2	3	4	5	6	7	8	9	10	11	12	13	14	15	16	17	18	19	20	21	22	23	24	25
4	F	1	2	3	4	5	6	7	8	9	10	11	12	13	14	15	16	17	18	19	20	21	22	23	24	25
4	G	1	2	3	4	5	6	7	8	9	10	11	12	13	14	15	16	17	18	19	20	21	22	23	24	25
5	H	1	2	3	4	5	6	7	8	9	10	11	12	13	14	15	16	17	18	19	20	21	22	23	24	25
5	I	1	2	3	4	5	6	7	8	9	10	11	12	13	14	15	16	17	18	19	20	21	22	23	24	25
5	J	1	2	3	4	5	6	7	8	9	10	11	12	13	14	15	16	17	18	19	20	21	22	23	24	25
6	K	1	2	3	4	5	6	7	8	9	10	11	12	13	14	15	16	17	18	19	20	21	22	23	24	25
6	L	1	2	3	4	5	6	7	8	9	10	11	12	13	14	15	16	17	18	19	20	21	22	23	24	25
7	M	1	2	3	4	5	6	7	8	9	10	11	12	13	14	15	16	17	18	19	20	21	22	23	24	25
7	N	1	2	3	4	5	6	7	8	9	10	11	12	13	14	15	16	17	18	19	20	21	22	23	24	25
8	O	1	2	3	4	5	6	7	8	9	10	11	12	13	14	15	16	17	18	19	20	21	22	23	24	25
8	P	1	2	3	4	5	6	7	8	9	10	11	12	13	14	15	16	17	18	19	20	21	22	23	24	25
9	Q	1	2	3	4	5	6	7	8	9	10	11	12	13	14	15	16	17	18	19	20	21	22	23	24	25
9	R	1	2	3	4	5	6	7	8	9	10	11	12	13	14	15	16	17	18	19	20	21	22	23	24	25
10	S	1	2	3	4	5	6	7	8	9	10	11	12	13	14	15	16	17	18	19	20	21	22	23	24	25
10	T	1	2	3	4	5	6	7	8	9	10	11	12	13	14	15	16	17	18	19	20	21	22	23	24	25

As individual stock prices change, so does the market capitalization of each company. The market is an ever-evolving pricing mechanism. This implies that smaller companies may grow to become larger companies and larger companies may decline in value and become smaller companies.

The evolution of rising and falling share values is analogous to a lava lamp. At the top of the lamp are the large companies and at the bottom are the small ones. Over time, the larger companies' growth prospects may cool, resulting in declining share values and declining market values. The smaller companies may experience rapid growth prospects, and be rewarded with rising share values, and hence increased market capitalizations.

It's important to recognize that small stocks and large stocks have various levels of real and perceived risk that can affect returns over time. This will be examined in the evaluation of the size premium in Appendix 2.

MARKET CAPITALIZATION

The sample stock market can be organized by the size, or market capitalization, of each company. A1 is the largest company, while T25 would represent the smallest company. Market capitalization is often shortened to "market cap" or "cap weight."

Market capitalization is the number of shares times the price per share. For example:

- A10, a large company, may have 300 million shares outstanding at $70 per share. This implies that the company has a market cap or market value of 300M x $70 = $21 billion. Assume that A10 represents 2.5% of the market.
- M7, a smaller company, may have 90 million shares trading at $10 per share. This implies that the company has a market cap or market value of 90M x $10 = $900 million. Assume that M7 represents 0.10% of the market.

Market capitalization of stocks in the market is often ranked by deciles. For example:

- Decile 1 and 2 would be considered large cap.
    - The 75 largest companies represent 64% of the market value.
- Decile 3 and 4 would be considered be mid cap.
    - The 100 mid cap companies represent 21% of the market value.
- Decile 5 to 10 would be considered be small cap and microcap.
    - The 325 small cap companies represent 15% of the market value.

Market capitalization and risk and return is examined in more detail in Appendix 2.

Figure 6.2: The sample stock market sorted by market capitalization or size

Decile	Large																								Large	% of market
1 A	1	2	3	4	5	6	7	8	9	10	11	12	13	14	15	16	17	18	19	20	21	22	23	24	25	
2 B	1	2	3	4	5	6	7	8	9	10	11	12	13	14	15	16	17	18	19	20	21	22	23	24	25	
2 C	1	2	3	4	5	6	7	8	9	10	11	12	13	14	15	16	17	18	19	20	21	22	23	24	25	64%
3 D	1	2	3	4	5	6	7	8	9	10	11	12	13	14	15	16	17	18	19	20	21	22	23	24	25	
3 E	1	2	3	4	5	6	7	8	9	10	11	12	13	14	15	16	17	18	19	20	21	22	23	24	25	
4 F	1	2	3	4	5	6	7	8	9	10	11	12	13	14	15	16	17	18	19	20	21	22	23	24	25	
4 G	1	2	3	4	5	6	7	8	9	10	11	12	13	14	15	16	17	18	19	20	21	22	23	24	25	21%
5 H	1	2	3	4	5	6	7	8	9	10	11	12	13	14	15	16	17	18	19	20	21	22	23	24	25	
5 I	1	2	3	4	5	6	7	8	9	10	11	12	13	14	15	16	17	18	19	20	21	22	23	24	25	
5 J	1	2	3	4	5	6	7	8	9	10	11	12	13	14	15	16	17	18	19	20	21	22	23	24	25	
6 K	1	2	3	4	5	6	7	8	9	10	11	12	13	14	15	16	17	18	19	20	21	22	23	24	25	
6 L	1	2	3	4	5	6	7	8	9	10	11	12	13	14	15	16	17	18	19	20	21	22	23	24	25	
7 M	1	2	3	4	5	6	7	8	9	10	11	12	13	14	15	16	17	18	19	20	21	22	23	24	25	
7 N	1	2	3	4	5	6	7	8	9	10	11	12	13	14	15	16	17	18	19	20	21	22	23	24	25	
8 O	1	2	3	4	5	6	7	8	9	10	11	12	13	14	15	16	17	18	19	20	21	22	23	24	25	
8 P	1	2	3	4	5	6	7	8	9	10	11	12	13	14	15	16	17	18	19	20	21	22	23	24	25	
9 Q	1	2	3	4	5	6	7	8	9	10	11	12	13	14	15	16	17	18	19	20	21	22	23	24	25	
9 R	1	2	3	4	5	6	7	8	9	10	11	12	13	14	15	16	17	18	19	20	21	22	23	24	25	
10 S	1	2	3	4	5	6	7	8	9	10	11	12	13	14	15	16	17	18	19	20	21	22	23	24	25	
10 T	1	2	3	4	5	6	7	8	9	10	11	12	13	14	15	16	17	18	19	20	21	22	23	24	25	15%
Small																									Small	100%

VALUE AND GROWTH CATEGORIZATION

Stocks can also be categorized as **growth stocks**, **value stocks**, or **blend.** Stocks categorized as "blend" can be considered to be priced at a fair value that precludes them from being specifically a growth stock or value stock. Growth stocks have a high share price relative to standard measures of valuation, and value stocks have a lower share price relative to standard measures of valuation.

Growth stocks are those that are expected to have better-than-average earnings growth over the long term. Growth stocks tend to see their shares trade at higher multiples to their book, sales, earnings, or cash flow per share, relative to the market, to reflect these expectations. Growth investors are willing to pay more for a company's shares relative to their intrinsic value, as they expect the company's recent fast-growing earnings will continue indefinitely.

Value stocks are those that are expected to have low or mediocre expected future earnings growth. Value companies tend to see their share prices trade at a lower multiple of their book value, sales, earnings, or cash flow per share, relative to the market, to reflect these expectations. Value investors invest in companies at a price that's low relative to their intrinsic value. Value investors attempt to buy shares at bargain price and wait for the market to realize that the stocks are worth more than what they're trading for, and drive up the price to its fair value.

Blend represents companies that exhibit valuation characteristics that cannot be clearly defined as growth or value.

It is important to recognize that it is the "expected growth" in earnings, sales, and so on, rather than historical growth, that affects investors' views, and hence, the stock valuation. Value stocks and growth stocks have various levels of real and perceived risk that can affect returns over time.

Value and growth relative to risk and return is examined in more detail in Appendix 3.

Figure 6.3: The sample stock market sorted by value, blend, and growth

Decile	Large Value									Blend												Large Growth				% of market
1 A	1	2	3	4	5	6	7	8	9	10	11	12	13	14	15	16	17	18	19	20	21	22	23	24	25	
2 B	1	2	3	4	5	6	7	8	9	10	11	12	13	14	15	16	17	18	19	20	21	22	23	24	25	
2 C	1	2	3	4	5	6	7	8	9	10	11	12	13	14	15	16	17	18	19	20	21	22	23	24	25	64%
3 D	1	2	3	4	5	6	7	8	9	10	11	12	13	14	15	16	17	18	19	20	21	22	23	24	25	
3 E	1	2	3	4	5	6	7	8	9	10	11	12	13	14	15	16	17	18	19	20	21	22	23	24	25	
4 F	1	2	3	4	5	6	7	8	9	10	11	12	13	14	15	16	17	18	19	20	21	22	23	24	25	
4 G	1	2	3	4	5	6	7	8	9	10	11	12	13	14	15	16	17	18	19	20	21	22	23	24	25	21%
5 H	1	2	3	4	5	6	7	8	9	10	11	12	13	14	15	16	17	18	19	20	21	22	23	24	25	
5 I	1	2	3	4	5	6	7	8	9	10	11	12	13	14	15	16	17	18	19	20	21	22	23	24	25	
5 J	1	2	3	4	5	6	7	8	9	10	11	12	13	14	15	16	17	18	19	20	21	22	23	24	25	
6 K	1	2	3	4	5	6	7	8	9	10	11	12	13	14	15	16	17	18	19	20	21	22	23	24	25	
6 L	1	2	3	4	5	6	7	8	9	10	11	12	13	14	15	16	17	18	19	20	21	22	23	24	25	
7 M	1	2	3	4	5	6	7	8	9	10	11	12	13	14	15	16	17	18	19	20	21	22	23	24	25	
7 N	1	2	3	4	5	6	7	8	9	10	11	12	13	14	15	16	17	18	19	20	21	22	23	24	25	
8 O	1	2	3	4	5	6	7	8	9	10	11	12	13	14	15	16	17	18	19	20	21	22	23	24	25	
8 P	1	2	3	4	5	6	7	8	9	10	11	12	13	14	15	16	17	18	19	20	21	22	23	24	25	
9 Q	1	2	3	4	5	6	7	8	9	10	11	12	13	14	15	16	17	18	19	20	21	22	23	24	25	
9 R	1	2	3	4	5	6	7	8	9	10	11	12	13	14	15	16	17	18	19	20	21	22	23	24	25	
10 S	1	2	3	4	5	6	7	8	9	10	11	12	13	14	15	16	17	18	19	20	21	22	23	24	25	
10 T	1	2	3	4	5	6	7	8	9	10	11	12	13	14	15	16	17	18	19	20	21	22	23	24	25	15%
	Small Value									Blend												Small Growth				100%

The market is an ever-evolving pricing mechanism. As individual stock prices change, so does their categorization of growth and value. A low-priced value stock could see a recovery in its business, and a corresponding increase in the share price, resulting in the transformation from a value stock to a growth stock. High-priced growth companies may see their share prices decline, resulting in a transformation from growth to value.

EXAMPLE 6.3: GROWTH GONE VALUE

In the later part of 2022, Russell, the data provider to the Russell indices, reclassified Meta (formerly Facebook, the "F" in FAANG) and Netflix (the "N") from growth to value during the index provider's annual reconstitution event. Although signs have been pointing to the waning dominance of FAANG stocks since the start of 2022, it is somewhat ironic that 40 percent of the pillars of the past growth stocks are now reclassified as value.

Equity Style Box

The Morningstar Equity Style Box™ was introduced in 1992 to help evaluate the equity style of an investment approach or fund. The Equity Style evaluates a portfolio holding relative to a specified category. Size is displayed along the vertical access. Large stocks at the top and small at the bottom. Price to valuation—that is, growth or value—is displayed along the horizontal access. Value is on the left, and growth is on the right.

Figure 6.4: Equity Style Box

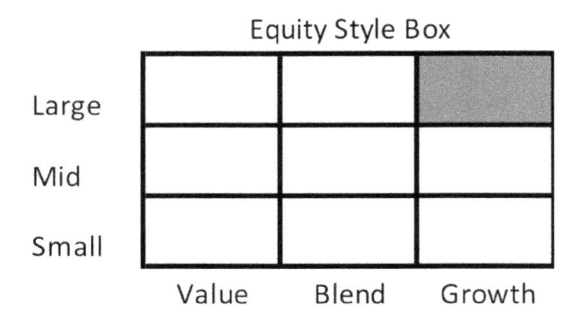

Equity Style Box

	Value	Blend	Growth
Large			■
Mid			
Small			

As an example, the above Equity Style Box indicates that the portfolio being analyzed holds most of its investments in large cap growth stocks.

TAKEAWAYS:

- Markets represent publicly traded companies.
- Markets are relatively efficient at pricing company valuation.
- Stocks can be sorted by size or market capitalization of the company.
- Stocks can be sorted as growth stocks, value stocks, or blend stocks.

Chapter 7
Capturing Return and Managing Risk

Efficient and effective investment management adds value over time

Investing, as noted throughout the book, is a series of decisions related to risk, return, time, and odds. The primary goal of investment management is to capture the return and manage the risk of a specific market or asset class. In chapter 6, as represented by figure 6.1, I introduced the hypothetical sample stock market containing 500 publicly traded companies. Assume you are given the task of efficiently and effectively capturing the return and managing the risk of the sample stock market.

The solution to accomplish this task has been debated and researched for decades.

Investment management has two distinct approaches

There are two distinct approaches to investment management that are commonly referred to as "passive" and "active" management. Passive management calls for holding highly diversified portfolios without expending effort or other resources attempting to improve investment performance through security analysis. Active management is the attempt to improve performance, either by identifying mispriced securities or by timing the performance of broad asset classes.

A third approach is often referred to as "semi-passive," and is commonly called "asset class" investing. Decades of theoretical and empirical research have shown that not all stocks have the same expected returns. Stated simply, investors demand higher returns to hold some stocks and lower returns to hold others. Semi-passive investment management techniques can design portfolios relative to a passive benchmark, to over-weight stocks with higher expected returns and under-weight stocks with lower expected returns.

In summary, there are three types of investment management:

1) **Active investment management**
   a. **Active – concentrated portfolio of stocks**
   b. **Active – investment manager (fund) portfolio of stocks**
2) **Passive (benchmark index) investment management**
3) **Semi-passive (asset class) investment management**

ACTIVE INVESTMENT MANAGEMENT

Active investment management is the conventional approach to investing. As its name implies, it takes a hands-on approach and requires that someone act on predictions and historical information to find the right stocks to buy, to sell, or to ignore. The goal of active money management is to beat the stock market's average returns and take full advantage of short-term price fluctuations. The "active" definition implies that the investor is making active assumptions based on changing information to determine which stocks they think will go up, and which stocks they think will go down. "Buy low, sell high" is the standard mantra for active investors. The challenge with making predictions about the future is that investors, to implement a profitable trading strategy, must not only predict future events, but must also predict how markets will react to those future events.

Active investment management:

- Attempts to identify mispricing in securities,
- Relies on forecasting to select "undervalued" securities or time markets,
- Generates higher expenses and trading costs and adds risk,
- Buys and sells investments based on changing perceptions.

Active investment management can be highly entertaining and is often the focus of media attention. It is human nature to select one item over another, if framed in a certain way. Active managers may utilize fundamental analysis, technical analysis, or a combination of the two, to forecast a stock's or market's next move.

FUNDAMENTAL ANALYSIS

Fundamental analysis is a method of measuring a security's intrinsic value by examining related economic and financial factors. Fundamental analysis examines anything that can affect the security's value, from macroeconomic factors such as the state of the economy and industry conditions to microeconomic factors like the effectiveness of the company's management. The goal is to form an opinion about whether the security is undervalued or overvalued.

TECHNICAL ANALYSIS

Technical analysis is a discipline employed to evaluate investments and identify trading opportunities in price trends and patterns seen on charts. Technical analysts believe past trading activity and price changes of a security can be valuable indicators of the security's future price movements.

ACTIVE—CONCENTRATED PORTFOLIO OF STOCKS

Active investors holding individual stocks tend to hold high-conviction portfolios. For example, let's assume an investor, after some research, has selected the following portfolio of twenty stocks, as represented by the shaded boxes in figure 7.1 The biggest company in the portfolio is company A2, and the smallest is F12.

Figure 7.1: The sample stock market with 20 stocks selected

Decile		Large Value										Blend										Large Growth			
1	A	1	2	3	4	5	6	7	8	9	10	11	12	13	14	15	16	17	18	19	20	21	22	23	24	25
2	B	1	2	3	4	5	6	7	8	9	10	11	12	13	14	15	16	17	18	19	20	21	22	23	24	25
2	C	1	2	3	4	5	6	7	8	9	10	11	12	13	14	15	16	17	18	19	20	21	22	23	24	25
3	D	1	2	3	4	5	6	7	8	9	10	11	12	13	14	15	16	17	18	19	20	21	22	23	24	25
3	E	1	2	3	4	5	6	7	8	9	10	11	12	13	14	15	16	17	18	19	20	21	22	23	24	25
4	F	1	2	3	4	5	6	7	8	9	10	11	12	13	14	15	16	17	18	19	20	21	22	23	24	25
4	G	1	2	3	4	5	6	7	8	9	10	11	12	13	14	15	16	17	18	19	20	21	22	23	24	25
5	H	1	2	3	4	5	6	7	8	9	10	11	12	13	14	15	16	17	18	19	20	21	22	23	24	25
5	I	1	2	3	4	5	6	7	8	9	10	11	12	13	14	15	16	17	18	19	20	21	22	23	24	25
5	J	1	2	3	4	5	6	7	8	9	10	11	12	13	14	15	16	17	18	19	20	21	22	23	24	25
6	K	1	2	3	4	5	6	7	8	9	10	11	12	13	14	15	16	17	18	19	20	21	22	23	24	25
6	L	1	2	3	4	5	6	7	8	9	10	11	12	13	14	15	16	17	18	19	20	21	22	23	24	25
7	M	1	2	3	4	5	6	7	8	9	10	11	12	13	14	15	16	17	18	19	20	21	22	23	24	25
7	N	1	2	3	4	5	6	7	8	9	10	11	12	13	14	15	16	17	18	19	20	21	22	23	24	25
8	O	1	2	3	4	5	6	7	8	9	10	11	12	13	14	15	16	17	18	19	20	21	22	23	24	25
8	P	1	2	3	4	5	6	7	8	9	10	11	12	13	14	15	16	17	18	19	20	21	22	23	24	25
9	Q	1	2	3	4	5	6	7	8	9	10	11	12	13	14	15	16	17	18	19	20	21	22	23	24	25
9	R	1	2	3	4	5	6	7	8	9	10	11	12	13	14	15	16	17	18	19	20	21	22	23	24	25
10	S	1	2	3	4	5	6	7	8	9	10	11	12	13	14	15	16	17	18	19	20	21	22	23	24	25
10	T	1	2	3	4	5	6	7	8	9	10	11	12	13	14	15	16	17	18	19	20	21	22	23	24	25
		Small Value										Blend										Small Growth			

An investor may believe they have selected the right companies, but they won't know until the future provides confirmation. How does one know the selected portfolio of companies will capture returns (go up) or create a loss by going down? Advisors may say they worked long hours researching which stocks to buy and which to sell.

> "The stock market does not care how hard you try."
> —Morgan Housel

The odds of you picking the right twenty stocks and avoiding the wrong twenty stocks is, from a statistical perspective, not great. There is nothing wrong with this approach, other than statistical odds. A selection of individual stocks reduces the consistency and reliability of outcomes. From the perspective of the *7 Steps to a Better Portfolio*, you are taking more risk, and you may not be compensated with added returns.

Historically, some investors, like Warren Buffet, have had great success with this approach. We know it is possible to have a successful concentrated portfolio, but is not probable for most investors.

ACTIVE—INVESTMENT MANAGER (FUND) PORTFOLIO OF STOCKS

A second form of active management is to hire one or more managers to select stocks for you. This can be done with:

- Actively managed mutual funds
- Separately managed accounts (SMA) of individual stocks
- Actively managed exchange-traded funds (ETF)

Actively managed funds are professionally managed portfolios that may have either specific or broad investment objectives. For the sake of example, we will assume they hold fifty stocks. Actively managed funds, although concentrated on the managers' top picks, are more diversified than a selection of just twenty stocks. In addition, most investors will hold several active funds to build out their portfolio.

The problem is how does the investor know if their fund manager has selected the right stocks, and if the next period's portfolio return will be as good as the last one? In addition, how do you know in the present which investment manager will outperform the market in the future? The commonly known and required disclosure on fund performance literature is "past performance is not an indication of future performance."

> "There is a strong probability that the hot manager of today will be the cold manager of tomorrow, or at least the day after tomorrow, and vice versa."
> —Peter Bernstein

Let's assume that an investment manager, after some research, has selected the following portfolio of fifty stocks, as represented by the shaded boxes in figure 7.2. The biggest company in the portfolio is company A1 and smallest is J20.

Figure 7.2: The sample stock market with 50 stocks selected

Decile		Large Value												Blend									Large Growth			
1	A	1	2	3	4	5	6	7	8	9	10	11	12	13	14	15	16	17	18	19	20	21	22	23	24	25
2	B	1	2	3	4	5	6	7	8	9	10	11	12	13	14	15	16	17	18	19	20	21	22	23	24	25
2	C	1	2	3	4	5	6	7	8	9	10	11	12	13	14	15	16	17	18	19	20	21	22	23	24	25
3	D	1	2	3	4	5	6	7	8	9	10	11	12	13	14	15	16	17	18	19	20	21	22	23	24	25
3	E	1	2	3	4	5	6	7	8	9	10	11	12	13	14	15	16	17	18	19	20	21	22	23	24	25
4	F	1	2	3	4	5	6	7	8	9	10	11	12	13	14	15	16	17	18	19	20	21	22	23	24	25
4	G	1	2	3	4	5	6	7	8	9	10	11	12	13	14	15	16	17	18	19	20	21	22	23	24	25
5	H	1	2	3	4	5	6	7	8	9	10	11	12	13	14	15	16	17	18	19	20	21	22	23	24	25
5	I	1	2	3	4	5	6	7	8	9	10	11	12	13	14	15	16	17	18	19	20	21	22	23	24	25
5	J	1	2	3	4	5	6	7	8	9	10	11	12	13	14	15	16	17	18	19	20	21	22	23	24	25
6	K	1	2	3	4	5	6	7	8	9	10	11	12	13	14	15	16	17	18	19	20	21	22	23	24	25
6	L	1	2	3	4	5	6	7	8	9	10	11	12	13	14	15	16	17	18	19	20	21	22	23	24	25
7	M	1	2	3	4	5	6	7	8	9	10	11	12	13	14	15	16	17	18	19	20	21	22	23	24	25
7	N	1	2	3	4	5	6	7	8	9	10	11	12	13	14	15	16	17	18	19	20	21	22	23	24	25
8	O	1	2	3	4	5	6	7	8	9	10	11	12	13	14	15	16	17	18	19	20	21	22	23	24	25
8	P	1	2	3	4	5	6	7	8	9	10	11	12	13	14	15	16	17	18	19	20	21	22	23	24	25
9	Q	1	2	3	4	5	6	7	8	9	10	11	12	13	14	15	16	17	18	19	20	21	22	23	24	25
9	R	1	2	3	4	5	6	7	8	9	10	11	12	13	14	15	16	17	18	19	20	21	22	23	24	25
10	S	1	2	3	4	5	6	7	8	9	10	11	12	13	14	15	16	17	18	19	20	21	22	23	24	25
10	T	1	2	3	4	5	6	7	8	9	10	11	12	13	14	15	16	17	18	19	20	21	22	23	24	25
		Small Value												Blend									Small Growth			

Active investment managers are just stock selectors, using the same information as all other investment specialists. Some will pick the correct stocks, and some will not. In the competitive and noisy world of investing, the random victors and losers make for great stories.

The markets aren't getting any greener! Why is my portfolio not moving?

Active management can be frustrating when markets are doing well and one's stocks or active funds are not. This is explained below in "why is it so hard to beat an index?"

PASSIVE (BENCHMARK INDEX) INVESTMENT MANAGEMENT

Passive investment management is also called index investment management. A portfolio is created to passively match or track the components of a financial market index, such as the Standard & Poor's 500 Index (S&P 500). A passive approach assumes that conventional index benchmarks are the best representation of a given market. Index funds can also be designed to track a specific industry sector, such has the S&P/TSX Capped Energy Index. Index funds can be in the form of a mutual fund or an exchange-traded fund (ETF).

An index is defined by a commercial index provider like Standard and Poor's (S&P). In fact, the largest and most popular index funds in the world are based around the S&P 500 index. There are numerous third-party index managers that offer S&P 500 index funds. An index provider does not use an entire stock market, but rather a defined list meeting some set of criteria. The index manager then attempts to buy and hold all the positions in proportion to the stated index market weights in an attempt to match or closely replicate that list. Whenever these indices switch up their constituents, the index managers that follow them are required to switch up their holdings by selling the stock that's leaving and buying the stock that's becoming part of the index. This trading activity and any costs of the fund create tracking errors between the stated index return and the actual return of the index fund. It is very important that investors realize that, due to tracking error, posted index returns are not the same as actual index fund returns.

Passive investment management:

- Allows the commercial index to determine the strategy,
- Attempts to match index performance, restricting which securities to hold and when to trade,
- Prioritizes low tracking error over higher expected returns,
- Focuses on the benefits of low cost.

Let's assume, for example, that A&B Co is a financial reporting company, like Dow Jones or Standard and Poor's, and has created an index benchmark using 250 of the largest and most liquid companies representing the 500 stocks in the sample stock market. Now let's assume that the 123-Investment Management Company, which creates index funds, creates the A&B 250 index fund and invests in all 250 companies, as represented by the shaded boxes in figure 7.3, in the same proportion as the reported index. 123-Investment Management Company will incur costs to manage this index fund that will impact the net return to investors. Let's assume that, like most indices, this is a market cap-weighted index. The larger companies will hold a larger weight in the index than the small companies. For example, A4 is a large company and J4 is one of the smaller companies held in the index fund.

Figure 7.3: The A&B 250 Index fund would hold the largest 250 stocks in the sample stock market

Decile		Large Value									Blend											Large Growth			
1	A	1	2	3	4	5	6	7	8	9	10	11	12	13	14	15	16	17	18	19	20	21	22	23	24	25
2	B	1	2	3	4	5	6	7	8	9	10	11	12	13	14	15	16	17	18	19	20	21	22	23	24	25
2	C	1	2	3	4	5	6	7	8	9	10	11	12	13	14	15	16	17	18	19	20	21	22	23	24	25
3	D	1	2	3	4	5	6	7	8	9	10	11	12	13	14	15	16	17	18	19	20	21	22	23	24	25
3	E	1	2	3	4	5	6	7	8	9	10	11	12	13	14	15	16	17	18	19	20	21	22	23	24	25
4	F	1	2	3	4	5	6	7	8	9	10	11	12	13	14	15	16	17	18	19	20	21	22	23	24	25
4	G	1	2	3	4	5	6	7	8	9	10	11	12	13	14	15	16	17	18	19	20	21	22	23	24	25
5	H	1	2	3	4	5	6	7	8	9	10	11	12	13	14	15	16	17	18	19	20	21	22	23	24	25
5	I	1	2	3	4	5	6	7	8	9	10	11	12	13	14	15	16	17	18	19	20	21	22	23	24	25
5	J	1	2	3	4	5	6	7	8	9	10	11	12	13	14	15	16	17	18	19	20	21	22	23	24	25
6	K	1	2	3	4	5	6	7	8	9	10	11	12	13	14	15	16	17	18	19	20	21	22	23	24	25
6	L	1	2	3	4	5	6	7	8	9	10	11	12	13	14	15	16	17	18	19	20	21	22	23	24	25
7	M	1	2	3	4	5	6	7	8	9	10	11	12	13	14	15	16	17	18	19	20	21	22	23	24	25
7	N	1	2	3	4	5	6	7	8	9	10	11	12	13	14	15	16	17	18	19	20	21	22	23	24	25
8	O	1	2	3	4	5	6	7	8	9	10	11	12	13	14	15	16	17	18	19	20	21	22	23	24	25
8	P	1	2	3	4	5	6	7	8	9	10	11	12	13	14	15	16	17	18	19	20	21	22	23	24	25
9	Q	1	2	3	4	5	6	7	8	9	10	11	12	13	14	15	16	17	18	19	20	21	22	23	24	25
9	R	1	2	3	4	5	6	7	8	9	10	11	12	13	14	15	16	17	18	19	20	21	22	23	24	25
10	S	1	2	3	4	5	6	7	8	9	10	11	12	13	14	15	16	17	18	19	20	21	22	23	24	25
10	T	1	2	3	4	5	6	7	8	9	10	11	12	13	14	15	16	17	18	19	20	21	22	23	24	25
		Small Value									Blend											Small Growth			

Why is it so hard to beat an index?

The primary reason index funds have an advantage over traditional active investment management is that many of the large indices have billions of dollars invested, do not require a large staff, and as a result, have low investment management costs.

There are two other factors at work that make it difficult to beat an index fund. First, there is the behavioral tendency to avoid betting on losers (every index will have stocks that are recent price decliners). Many losers that have fallen in value, statistically, become tomorrow's winners. Index funds, having no emotion, will still own them if they fit the benchmark criteria. Investment managers may, based on their expectations or presentation optics, sell off the losers. And second, the distribution of stock returns is heavily skewed, with a relatively small number of stocks providing a good chunk of the overall index's returns (active managers not owning those few winners may underperform the index). This is explained in the section "Needle in a haystack" in chapter 4. As a result of these two factors, some indices—most notably the S&P 500, which represents the large cap US companies—can be difficult to outperform.

Are index funds passive or active investment vehicles?

The increased popularity of index funds may not imply that investors are employing a buy and hold passive strategy. Some investors may use index funds to pursue an active investment approach. For example, the largest S&P 500 ETF had the highest average daily trade volume of US-listed securities in 2021, at $31 billion USD. It is reasonable to assume a portion of that trading activity represented asset allocation changes motivated by market viewpoints, rather than buy-and-hold position accumulation.

One index fund is not enough

Index funds investors should always consider global asset allocation. Investors who held most of their savings in the S&P 500 index fund during the "lost decade" of 2000–2009 would have seen an average return of -0.95 percent per year (US $ return). Over this same time, US value returned approximately 4 percent per year, US small cap returned almost 9 percent, international stocks around 10 percent, and emerging markets close to 11 percent. Holding a significant position of one's portfolio in the world's most famous index, holding large cap US stocks, would have been detrimental to investors' long-term returns.

Does the benchmark index best represent the market?

An index fund is an inexpensive way to capture the market returns of a broad group of stocks. But is the index an accurate benchmark for the market it seeks to represent?

Many of the world's most popular benchmark indices are market cap weighted, making them easily accessible to most investors to gain access to a well-diversified, broad-based portfolio. Over time, however, if certain companies grow enough, they can end up making up an excessive amount of the weighting in an index. This is because, as a company grows, index designers are obligated to appoint a greater percentage of the company to the index. These companies tend to be less volatile, more mature, and better suited for most investors as core holdings. At the same time, this effect can endanger a diversified index by placing too much weight on one individual stock's performance, as it comes to dominate the index makeup.

A passive investment approach is based around the "efficient market hypothesis." The term "efficient market hypothesis" essentially means that share prices fully reflect all available information. The markets may reflect all investors' views of information, but are all stocks effectively priced? The toughest challenge to the efficient market theory comes from behavioral finance research that indicates that some stocks may at times reflect the irrational emotions rather than rational analysis of available information. When greed and fear take over, stock prices may not be effectively priced. The euphoria that fueled the technology stock bubble in 1999 and 2000 is clear evidence of this phenomenon.

Another problem with indexing is that the commercial index provider determines the stocks or bonds held in the portfolio. The firm publishes a list—usually annually or semi-annually—containing all the stocks composing that index, or benchmark. The manager attempts to closely track the benchmark. But rigid construction works against the strategy. Most index fund managers are judged by their ability to closely track their respective index. The main problems with this approach are loss of control, trading disadvantage, and style drift.

Asset class funds, given that they look at an entire market and have more trading flexibility, may be considered a better vehicle than an index fund, to capture the returns and manage the risks.

Sector index funds

Sector index and exchange-traded funds are become increasingly popular among investors and have seen exponential growth in the past decade. A sector exchange-traded index fund (ETF) is a pooled investment vehicle that invests specifically in the stocks and securities of a particular industry or sector, typically identified in the fund's title. For instance, a sector ETF may track a representative basket of energy stocks or technology stocks. Sector index funds are often viewed as trading vehicles rather than passive long-term portfolio building blocks. These investment vehicles enable investors to trade more frequently than would be possible in a traditional mutual fund.

Actively managed exchange-traded funds are not index funds

The growth of financial technology has resulted in many traditional active investment management funds being traded as ETFs. The underlying concept behind an actively managed ETF is that a portfolio manager adjusts the investments within the fund as desired, while not being subject to the set rules of tracking an index—like a passively managed ETF attempts to do. Actively managed exchange-traded funds may experience large premiums or discounts to net asset value (NAV) in volatile trading days, and have higher expense ratios.

SEMI-PASSIVE (ASSET CLASS) INVESTMENT MANAGEMENT

Asset class investment management, an alternative approach to both conventional investment management and passive indexing, has benefited significantly from the numerous breakthroughs in the field of financial science over the last fifty-plus years. The academic research into valuation theory provided a framework for the drivers of expected stock returns. Valuation theory links expectations about a firm's future cash flows to its current value through a discount rate (or, equivalently, the expected return on the stock). Using the valuation framework, we can expect small cap stocks to outperform large cap stocks, low relative price stocks (value stocks) to outperform high relative price stocks (growth stocks), and stocks with higher profitability to outperform low profitability stocks. Consistent with valuation theory, the existence of these premiums has been documented in academic studies covering over forty countries and nine decades of stock data. Asset class managers will structure portfolios to target these dimensions to add value for their clients. The result is a broad market asset class portfolio that offers diversification across hundreds, if not thousands, of securities that target higher expected returns.

Asset class investment management uses valuation theory to divide the market into categories. Three categories, backed by empirical evidence, are often referred to as factors or dimensions of expected return:

- Company size / Size premium = Small versus large companies (Appendix 2)
- Relative price / Value premium = Value versus growth companies (Appendix 3)
- Profitability / Profitability premium = High versus low profitability companies (Appendix 4)

The asset class premiums will be examined in greater detail in their respective appendices.

An asset class fund is a thinking index

Index investment management is considered passive as it follows or matches a strategy determined by a commercial index provider. An index approach does not use or require any investment analysis; it simply attempts to replicate and match the commercial index performance.

Asset class investment management, on the other hand, is considered a semi-passive investment approach. An asset class fund, like an index fund, will hold a broad basket of stocks within a given market. However, asset class funds use academic research into the drivers of expected returns to include, exclude, under-weight, or over-weight portfolio holdings relative to a benchmark index. The research and portfolio construction can be used to increase the expected returns of a stock portfolio without having to try to outguess the market.

An asset class fund portfolio, like an index fund portfolio, is just 100 units that adds up to 100 percent. Individual holdings can constitute a large position, say 5 percent of the total portfolio or a small position, say 0.03 percent of the portfolio. An index fund, like our hypothetical A&B 250 index fund, has a set percent allocation to all 250 stocks. An asset class fund, while it may hold the same stocks as the index fund, will weight its allocation differently.

Portfolio weights of an asset class fund versus a benchmark index fund

The asset class fund will adjust its investment allocation weight relative to a benchmark index based on the three categories previously mentioned above. These are discussed in greater detail in Appendices 2, 3, and 4. See figures 7.4 and 7.5 for a visual of the asset class fund's over-weighting or under-weighting of stocks relative to a benchmark index fund.

1) **Adjust portfolio weights based on size—small versus large**
   The asset class fund will over-weight small stocks and under-weight large stocks, relative to the benchmark, to increase the expected return of the portfolio. The higher expected return for small companies is explained in Appendix 2.

   Under-weight large cap stock by **0.60%**

   - A22 is a large stock that represents 1.5% of the benchmark index. The asset class fund may only hold 0.90% of the stock. The asset class fund, focusing on higher expected returns, has under-weighted its portfolio relative to the benchmark index by 0.60%.

	Benchmark index	Asset class fund	Under-weight A22 large company shares
Weight %	1.5%	0.90%	0.60%

   Over-weight small cap stock by **0.10%**

   - H4 is a small stock that represents 0.05% of the benchmark index market. The asset class may hold 0.15% of the stock. The asset class fund, focusing on higher expected returns, has over-weighted its portfolio relative to the benchmark index by 0.10%.

	Benchmark index	Asset class fund	Over-weight H4 small company shares
Weight %	0.05%	0.15%	0.10%

2) **Adjust portfolio weights based on price—value versus growth**
   The asset class fund will over-weight value stocks and under-weight growth stocks, relative to the benchmark, to increase the expected return of the portfolio. The higher expected return for value companies is explained in Appendix 3.

   Under-weight growth stock by **0.11%**

   - E23 is a growth stock that represents 0.21% of the market. The asset class may only hold 0.10% of the stock. The asset class fund, focusing on higher expected returns, has under-weighted its portfolio relative to the benchmark index by 0.11%

	Benchmark index	Asset class fund	Under-weight E23 growth company shares
Weight %	0.21%	0.10%	0.11%

Over-weight value stock by **0.20%**

- E3 is a value stock that represents 0.30% of the market. The asset class may hold 0.50% of the stock. The asset class fund, focusing on higher expected returns, has over-weighted its portfolio relative to the benchmark index by 0.20%.

	Benchmark index	Asset class fund	Over-weight E3 value company shares
Weight %	0.30%	0.50%	0.20%

3) **Adjust portfolio weights based on profitability—high profitability versus low profitability**

An additional driver of higher expected return is the profitability premium, which will be further explained in Appendix 4. For now, think of the premium as an overlay to the portfolio construction process. The asset class fund will over-weight high profitability stocks and under-weight low profitability stocks, relative to the benchmark, to increase expected return of the portfolio.

Under-weight low profitability stock by **0.95%**

- C24 is a low profitability stock that represents 1.1% of the market. In addition to being a large and growth stock, the asset class may only hold 0.15% of the stock. The asset class fund, focusing on higher expected returns, has under-weighted its portfolio relative to the benchmark index by 0.95%.

	Benchmark index	Asset class fund	Under-weight C24 company that exhibits lower profitability
Weight %	1.10%	0.15%	0.95%

Over-weight high profitability by **0.20%**

- B17 is a high profitability stock that represents 2.1% of the market. In addition to being a large and growth stock, the overlay of higher profitability may result in the asset class fund holding 2.3% of the stock. The asset class fund, focusing on higher expected returns, has over-weighted its portfolio relative to the benchmark index by 0.20%.

	Benchmark index	Asset class fund	Over-weight B17 company that exhibits higher profitability
Weight %	2.10%	2.30%	0.20%

4) **Adjust weights for inclusion or exclusion versus the benchmark index**
   The asset class fund may add small stocks that may not be included in the benchmark index.

   Over-weight a small stock by **0.05%**

- N4 is a small value stock not held by the benchmark index. By adding the investment to the asset class fund, you are adding to the over-weighting of small value. The asset class fund, focusing on higher expected returns, has over-weighted its portfolio relative to the benchmark index by 0.05%.

	Benchmark index	Asset class fund	Over-weight small company shares
Weight %	0.00%	0.05%	0.05%

Asset class managers create semi-passive portfolios they believe are better focused on higher expected returns than the comparable benchmark indices. The portfolios will over-weight, relative to the benchmark index, company shares that exhibit better valuation, smaller market capitalization, and higher profitability. Assume that an asset class manager created a core fund holding 300 companies, as represented by the shaded boxes in figure 7.4. The biggest company in the portfolio is company A1, and the smallest is P5.

Figure 7.4: An asset class fund holding 300 stocks

Decile	Large Value												Blend									Large Growth			
1 A	1	2	3	4	5	6	7	8	9	10	11	12	13	14	15	16	17	18	19	20	21	22	23	24	25
2 B	1	2	3	4	5	6	7	8	9	10	11	12	13	14	15	16	17	18	19	20	21	22	23	24	25
2 C	1	2	3	4	5	6	7	8	9	10	11	12	13	14	15	16	17	18	19	20	21	22	23	24	25
3 D	1	2	3	4	5	6	7	8	9	10	11	12	13	14	15	16	17	18	19	20	21	22	23	24	25
3 E	1	2	3	4	5	6	7	8	9	10	11	12	13	14	15	16	17	18	19	20	21	22	23	24	25
4 F	1	2	3	4	5	6	7	8	9	10	11	12	13	14	15	16	17	18	19	20	21	22	23	24	25
4 G	1	2	3	4	5	6	7	8	9	10	11	12	13	14	15	16	17	18	19	20	21	22	23	24	25
5 H	1	2	3	4	5	6	7	8	9	10	11	12	13	14	15	16	17	18	19	20	21	22	23	24	25
5 I	1	2	3	4	5	6	7	8	9	10	11	12	13	14	15	16	17	18	19	20	21	22	23	24	25
5 J	1	2	3	4	5	6	7	8	9	10	11	12	13	14	15	16	17	18	19	20	21	22	23	24	25
6 K	1	2	3	4	5	6	7	8	9	10	11	12	13	14	15	16	17	18	19	20	21	22	23	24	25
6 L	1	2	3	4	5	6	7	8	9	10	11	12	13	14	15	16	17	18	19	20	21	22	23	24	25
7 M	1	2	3	4	5	6	7	8	9	10	11	12	13	14	15	16	17	18	19	20	21	22	23	24	25
7 N	1	2	3	4	5	6	7	8	9	10	11	12	13	14	15	16	17	18	19	20	21	22	23	24	25
8 O	1	2	3	4	5	6	7	8	9	10	11	12	13	14	15	16	17	18	19	20	21	22	23	24	25
8 P	1	2	3	4	5	6	7	8	9	10	11	12	13	14	15	16	17	18	19	20	21	22	23	24	25
9 Q	1	2	3	4	5	6	7	8	9	10	11	12	13	14	15	16	17	18	19	20	21	22	23	24	25
9 R	1	2	3	4	5	6	7	8	9	10	11	12	13	14	15	16	17	18	19	20	21	22	23	24	25
10 S	1	2	3	4	5	6	7	8	9	10	11	12	13	14	15	16	17	18	19	20	21	22	23	24	25
10 T	1	2	3	4	5	6	7	8	9	10	11	12	13	14	15	16	17	18	19	20	21	22	23	24	25

Small Value — Blend — Small Growth

Investment weights relative to benchmark:
- Over-weight the investment relative to the benchmark index
- Equal weight the investment relative to the benchmark index
- Under-weight the investment relative to the benchmark index

Figure 7.5: Summary of an asset class fund's over-weighting and under-weighting of stocks relative to a benchmark index

		Value	Blend	Growth	Total
Large Cap	Asset class fund	29%	16%	11%	56%
	Benchmark index	15%	21%	31%	67%
Mid Cap	Asset class fund	10%	9%	6%	25%
	Benchmark index	4%	8%	11%	23%
Small Cap	Asset class fund	13%	6%	0%	19%
	Benchmark index	2%	3%	5%	10%
	Asset class fund	52%	31%	17%	
	Benchmark index	21%	32%	47%	

The asset class fund will **over-weight** its portfolio allocation versus the benchmark:

- Large value   29% vs. 15%   over-weight by 14%
- Mid value   10% vs. 4%   over-weight by 6%
- Mid blend   9% vs. 8%   over-weight by 1%
- Small value   13% vs.2%   over-weight by 11%
- Small blend value   6% vs. 3%   over-weight by 3%

The asset class fund will **under-weight** its portfolio allocation versus the benchmark:

- Large growth   11% vs. 31%   under-weight 20%
- Large blend   16% vs. 21%   under-weight by 5%
- Mid growth   6% vs. 11%   under-weight by 5%
- Small growth   0% vs. 5%   under-weight by 5%

An asset class fund focused on the stocks with higher expected returns (Appendices 2, 3, and 4) is a well-diversified portfolio that makes a great portfolio building block. While the asset class fund seeks to outperform a market portfolio in many ways, returns are noisy and there can be periods of time when a particular premium does not deliver. The goal of an asset class fund is to help investors benefit from premiums when they are realized and offer market-like returns when they are not.

Dimensional Fund Advisors (DFA) is the largest provider of broad market-based multifactor asset class funds. www.dimensional.com

---

TAKEAWAYS:

- Portfolios holding a small number of individual stocks are considered high-conviction portfolios.
- Active investment managers holding their favorite selected stocks may lack diversification and may miss out potential returns.
- Passive / index investment management attempts to replicate a commercial index.
- Semi-passive / asset class is a thinking index that attempts to outperform an index by selectively over-weighting some index stocks and under-weighting others, based on expected returns.

Chapter 8

Three Portfolio Approaches

Different approaches have different risks, returns, and odds

A portfolio is only one hundred. By this I mean one hundred units, or 100 percent. Your choice of investment vehicles, and how much you allocate to your portfolio, can have a material impact on portfolio risk and return. Each investment vehicle you add to your portfolio is responsible for capturing future returns and managing the risks to provide the best odds of long-term portfolio success.

Three portfolio approaches

Investors have endless investment choices. A good starting point is to narrow the portfolio methods down to the three approaches:

1) Portfolio of individual stocks (active investment management)
2) Portfolio of active mutual funds or managers (active investment management)
3) Portfolio of index and asset class funds (passive and semi-passive investment management

There are significant risk and reward trade-offs when choosing any of the three portfolio approaches. Investing in individual stocks can result in the thrill of victory or the agony of defeat. Active managers can be superstars or metaphorically drive your portfolio into the ditch. Some investors may find index and asset class funds, which evolve with changing asset prices, too boring.

The objective of a portfolio is to capture return and manage risk to increase the odds of a successful investment experience

All the various investment and portfolio risks are discussed in these chapters and appendices. It's also important to note that all investing is subject to systematic risk. Systematic risk, also referred to as market risk, is the risk of a large macro event in which unexpected risks appear and the resulting uncertainty affects most asset prices in a negative way. Examples of systematic risks, as noted in chapter 3, include the 2008 global financial crisis, the uncertainty of COVID-19 in 2020, the conflict in Ukraine, and unexpected higher rate of inflation in 2022.

Each of the three portfolio approaches will be evaluated relative to the 7 Steps in an evaluation rubric in chapter 10. A rubric is a scoring guide commonly used in education to evaluate performance.

1. PORTFOLIO OF INDIVIDUAL STOCKS

The first approach is to select a portfolio of individual company shares (stocks). The selection of specific investments may be made by an advisor or the individual investor. This approach is referred to as active management and involves actively buying and selling stocks and bonds to enhance return. This approach relies on predictions and/or back-tested simulations, to find mispricing, to time markets. This type of portfolio holds between ten to forty individual stocks and bonds. This portfolio approach may fall into one of two categories:

1) RECOMMENDED STOCKS AND BONDS:

Stocks and bonds recommended by the investment firms and the media. They may have done well in recent years, and they feel good to own.

2) ASSORTMENT OF STOCKS AND BONDS:

Stocks and bonds with a reason to be placed in the portfolio. Once in the portfolio, one may forget why they ended up there and may not find a compelling reason to sell them.

Most investors end up holding a portfolio of assorted stocks.

Why do investors choose a portfolio of individual stocks?
- Owning individual companies can feel empowering.
- It can be a thrill when the investment appreciates in value.
- They believe in the management and the business.
- Recommended stocks feel comfortable to own.
- The dividend may be attractive.
- Familiarity with the company or industry.

What are the frustrations and risks with a portfolio of individual stocks?
- Picking stocks is hard and time-consuming and can be emotionally exhausting.
- All the research and conviction does not guarantee a successful investment outcome.

- Individual stocks can be very unpredictable.
- The stock value can decline without warning.
- The stock does not recover, and you give up.
- Research reports contradict what you think of the company.
- Management decisions can be frustrating.
- A "strong buy" recommendation does not mean it will go up.
- Confusion about what to do next.
- Falling for the illusion that someone picking stocks for you can see into the future.

Stock picking is human nature. Stock picking is like making a prediction in politics, sports, or the weather. By investing in a stock, we hope to validate our confidence in our choice. Stock picking suggests one can, not just randomly, but with persistence, pick better stocks than the collective wisdom of the market. Picking more winners than losers may seem doable on the surface, but the data would suggest otherwise.

One form of active investing investors may get involved in is referred to as "day trading." Day trading can be like playing a video game. Buy a symbol and sell a symbol. It's an intuitive game where you hope you are on the right side of the trade. The outcome is unpredictable and can be draining, both emotionally and financially.

Picking stocks is about what you want to happen, what is happening, what could happen, and what you control. Stock picking carries more uncertainty and decision-making issues. Stock picking may not compensate investors for the added risk.

EXAMPLE 8.1: LOVE, HATE, IGNORE

One of my favorite team projects for my undergraduate students, which illustrates the difficulty of picking individual stocks, was a team assignment called "Love Hate Ignore."

During the first week of my finance class, the teams and I would agree on ten commonly known companies that traded on either US or Canadian exchanges. The teams would research all ten companies. Teams would select three companies they estimated might appreciate the most. They would select three companies they estimate might decline the most over the next ten weeks of the class. We also tracked the returns of the four companies they decided to ignore.

1) Love: Invest $100,000 each in three of the companies they felt most confident would appreciate over the term of the course.

2) Hate: Short sell $100,000 each of the three companies they felt most confident would decline in value over the term of the course. Short selling implies selling shares you don't own (for example, selling them at $10/share) with the assumption you can purchase them at a lower price (for example, buying them at $7/share) in the future. The gain is the $7 cost to buy back the shares relative to the $10 proceeds from the sale (10 - 7 = $3 a share). An investor conducts a short sell when they believe the shares will decline in value.

3) Ignore: Neither purchase nor sell the shares of these four companies.

Each week the teams' "love, hate, ignore" portfolios' returns would be revealed and discussed. Love, Hate, Ignore is the ultimate voting example of how investors' perspectives impact what investments the love (buy), hate (sell), or ignore.

Appendix 1 has a simpler version of this game called "The Stock Picking Game."

2. PORTFOLIO OF ACTIVE MUTUAL FUNDS OR MANAGERS

The second approach is to select and manage a long-term portfolio of traditional active mutual funds and exchange-traded funds (ETFs). A mutual fund is a financial vehicle that pools together investors (called shareholders or unit holders) into a fund managed by professional investment managers. These funds are offered by banks and investment firms, and may include hedge funds and alternative investment strategies. This approach is also considered active management. The portfolio building blocks are a variety of actively managed investment funds.

This portfolio approach holds between four and ten individual, actively managed mutual funds, ETFs, or separately managed accounts (SMA). SMAs are like mutual funds, except rather than owning units in a fund, the investor holds all the individual stocks and bonds directly.

THIS PORTFOLIO APPROACH MAY FALL INTO ONE OF TWO CATEGORIES:

1) Portfolio of top active funds or managers:

Funds that may be recommended picks by the investment firms and the media. They may have done well in recent years, and they feel good to own.

2) Assortment of active funds or managers:

Once in the portfolio, one may forget why they ended up there and may not find a compelling reason to remove them.

Most investors end up holding a portfolio of assorted active mutual funds or managers.

Why do investors choose a portfolio of active mutual funds or managers?
- Selecting top-rated fund managers seems like an easy decision
- High expectations for future returns
- Added diversification over picking individual stocks

- High conviction in the skills of the investment manager
- High ratings, based on past performance, instills confidence
- Exciting to own top-rated managers

What are the frustrations and risks with a portfolio of active mutual funds or managers?

- Recent outperformance does not guarantee future outperformance. There is seldom persistent outperformance. The past outperforming managers may have done well due to unexpected events. When these unexpected events normalize in their chosen sector, many of these managers get caught and may suffer below-average portfolio returns.
- All the manager research does not guarantee successful investment outcomes.
- Fund returns may lag the market for long periods of time.
- Flashy, promising marketing doesn't deliver.
- Manager excuses for poor performance are annoying.
- Demoralizing, when prior winners lose so much of your money.
- High investment costs.
- Investor impatience may result in firing the manager at the wrong time.
- Falling for the illusion that fund managers can predict the future.

Picking the managers who will pick the next year's winning stocks can be hard. The past is not the future. The trap of chasing the past returns can lead to more risk and less return. Investors see past returns as an indicator of a high probability of future return. Unfortunately, that is not how it works.

3. PORTFOLIO OF INDEX AND ASSET CLASS FUNDS

The third approach in portfolio management is to select and manage a portfolio of index and asset class funds. This approach is a combination of passive (index) and semi-passive (asset class) investment funds.

BROAD-BASED INDEX FUND (PASSIVE)

Focus on matching the returns of a defined broad benchmark index, restricting which securities to hold and when to trade. One example is the Vanguard S&P 500 Index ETF.

SECTOR-BASED INDEX FUND (PASSIVE)

Focus on matching the returns of a defined sector benchmark index, restricting which securities to hold and when to trade. An example is a Canadian real estate or energy company index ETF.

BROAD-BASED ASSET CLASS FUND (SEMI-PASSIVE)

Starting with a broad market index, the manager reallocates market weights to increase weighting in areas of the market with higher expected returns. The manager adds more holdings in value and small cap companies, and reduces holdings in growth and large cap companies. Please see Chapter 7 and figure 7.4 and 7.5.

THIS PORTFOLIO APPROACH MAY FALL INTO ONE OF TWO CATEGORIES:

1) Portfolio of assorted index funds and asset class funds:

Index and asset class funds ended up in one's portfolio as a recommendation. The investor may not understand why it was bought or how it relates to other parts of their portfolio.

2) Globally allocated and broadly diversified portfolio of index and asset class funds:

A portfolio focused on global allocation and broad diversification is the ideal portfolio structure because it contains carefully selected index and asset class funds that, together, are designed to capture return and reduce portfolio risk.

7 Steps encourages investors to build and manage globally allocated, broadly diversified portfolios of index and asset class funds.

Why do investors choose a portfolio of index and asset class funds?

- Broad Index and asset class funds are designed to capture the returns of a designated benchmark.
- They are excellent building blocks to build a globally allocated portfolio.
- They are a less expensive form of investment management.
- This adds diversification over a portfolio of individual stocks or active investment funds.
- This is more rules based and process driven.

What are the frustrations and risks with a portfolio of index and asset class funds?

- A broader-based fund, like an index or asset class, may underperform various sector funds. When a given market return is dominated by a particular sector—for example, technology—investors may chase the temporary outperformance of the sector over the more diversified underperforming index or asset class approach.
- Some indices become dominated by a few stocks:
    - Canada was dominated by Shopify (2020s) and Nortel (1990s)
    - US large cap indices (2021) were dominated by the FAANG stocks (Facebook [now Meta], Amazon, Apple, Netflix, and Google [now Alphabet])
- Investors sell the underperforming index, only to see it reverse and outperform in the future

Index and asset class funds are excellent portfolio building blocks for long-term investors. The goal of *7 Steps* is to encourage the use of index and asset class funds as investment vehicles when building and managing a globally allocated, broadly diversified portfolio approach.

TAKEAWAYS:

- Investors have three distinct portfolio approaches to consider when seeking to capture return and manage risk.
- Active investment portfolios traditionally utilize stock picking and active manager selection.
- Passive and semi-passive investment portfolios tend to buy and hold index and asset class funds.
- There are risk and reward trade-offs when choosing any of the three portfolio approaches.

Chapter 9

7 Steps to a Better Portfolio

Steps in the right direction

7 Steps is a rules-based, systematic investment approach to help keep you focused on the variables you can control, to better manage the variables that you cannot. The 7 Steps encourage a process of critical thinking regarding the design, construction, investment selection, and management of a portfolio. The Steps provide a formulaic framework to evaluate the benefits and drawbacks of investment decisions. The Steps are like a road map to guide you through the endless noise and keep you focused on the journey ahead.

Focus on what you control to better manage what you don't

Successful, long-term investing will be determined by the quality of your decisions and the framework or structure with which to evaluate those decisions. The quality of your decisions will depend on what information is evidence based and what is opinion based. An intelligently structured, disciplined portfolio approach will provide consistency, help you manage variables, and reduce the impact of investment noise. Investment strategy is about the odds. You are tasked with employing an investment strategy that captures the returns and manages the risk of a given market to increase the odds of a successful long-term investment outcome.

Capturing returns and managing risk—7 Steps to a Better Portfolio

As discussed throughout this book, investors choose to invest for many reasons. As noted in chapter 3, the return investors seek is derived from accepting risk. The goal for portfolio investing is to capture the returns available, while managing the risks presented in the investing arena.

7 STEPS:

1) **Allocate across global capital markets**
2) **Diversify broadly within markets**

3) **Focus on higher expected returns**
4) **Utilize financial science**
5) **Manage strategy risk**
6) **Manage investment choice risk**
7) **Manage costs and taxes**

Each of the 7 Steps describes a controllable variable that, when consistently executed over time, will increase the probability of the intended outcome. Anything is possible, but successful investing, over time, is about probability. A rules-based, systematic approach can help keep you focused on the variables you can control. This results in better management of the variables to mitigate the risks that you cannot control. In a complicated, uncertain, and noisy investing world, it is important to use an approach that keeps you going in the right direction.

Rather than concentrate on each Step in isolation, the Steps should be viewed in the aggregate. The interrelationship among the steps creates synergies to enhance return and reduce portfolio risk.

Portfolio synergies => the whole is greater than the sum of its parts

Capturing return, managing risk, controlling emotions, and reducing costs and taxes will improve the odds of a successful, long-term investment experience. The more effective and efficient the investment approach is at capturing available investment returns, the greater the impact of compounding wealth.

STEP 1: ALLOCATE ACROSS GLOBAL CAPITAL MARKETS

Asset allocation has long been considered one of the most important decisions an investor can make. In fact, asset allocation is likely to have a bigger impact on the performance of a portfolio than the selection of individual investments. Asset allocation is the implementation of an investment strategy that attempts to balance risk and reward by adjusting the percentage of each asset in an investment portfolio.

Think of your portfolio as seven cups to allocate your investments across. Think of your investments as a jug of money equal to 100 percent. Your task is to allocate this 100 percent across seven cups:

1) Global bonds (fixed income)
2) Canada equity
3) US equity
4) International equity
5) Emerging markets equity
6) Other equity (specific to the opportunity)
7) Global real estate equity

Portfolio 100%

The first decision is the allocation between fixed income (bonds) and stocks (equity) by deciding which percentage of assets should be invested in lower-risk bonds versus higher-risk equities. Fixed income can serve many roles in a portfolio to help investors achieve their goals, including managing overall portfolio volatility and managing future cash flow requirements. For example, adding fixed income to an equity portfolio is one of the most effective tools an investor can use to balance the expected volatility and returns of the total portfolio. Equity holdings may outperform one year, while bonds could do better the next. Therefore, a sensible portfolio should have a mix of these two major asset classes. Low risk, fixed income is also good for cash flow planning. Assume a portfolio is $100 and the investor needs to withdraw $3.40 or 3.4 percent from the portfolio each year. The investor can allocate $17 or 17 percent to low-risk bonds to plan for five years of cash flow requirements. Managing for future cash flow needs is common in pension fund management. In addition to cash flow needs, determining the appropriate amount of fixed income to include in a portfolio should be based on an investor's goals, risk tolerance, preferences, time frame, and any other constraints.

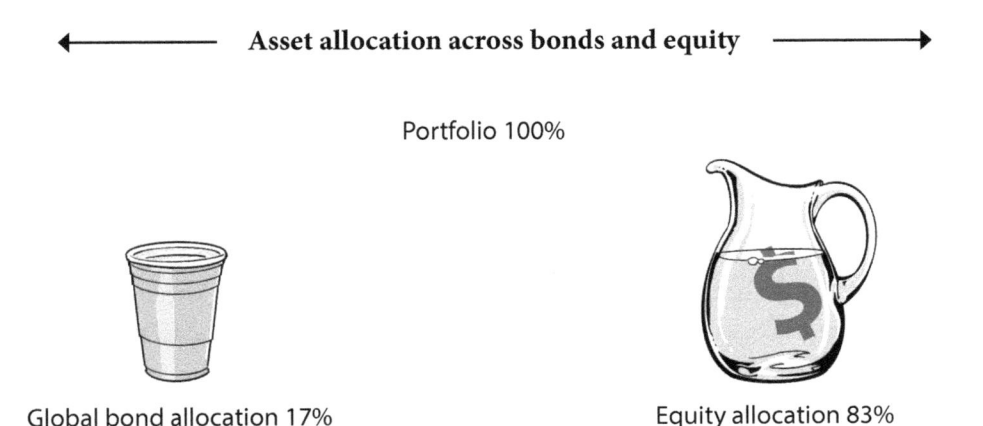

⟵ **Asset allocation across bonds and equity** ⟶

Portfolio 100%

Global bond allocation 17%   Equity allocation 83%

The next decision is the allocation across the global equity markets. Investment opportunities exist all around the ever-evolving global capital markets. It's hard to know where next year's best returns will appear. A globally allocated portfolio can help capture a broad range of returns and deliver more reliable outcomes over time. Think of global allocation as breadth across the global markets.

Equity allocation 83%

← Asset allocation across the global markets →

| Canada equity 21% | US equity 24% | International equity 16% | Emerging mkts equity 9% | Other equity 5% | Global real estate 8% |

Global allocation is an effective way to manage country-specific risk. It also provides a good rationale for investors to hold the equity and fixed income securities of firms across developed and emerging markets, in addition to investing in their own market. While each of the regions offers the potential to earn positive expected returns in the long run, they may perform quite differently over short periods. There is no reliable evidence that the performance of one country or region relative to another can be predicted in advance.

Every publicly traded company belongs to an investment category. The first category is country. The Morgan Stanley Composite Index (MSCI) Global Investable Market Indexes (GIMI) is organized into developed, emerging, and frontier markets. Frontier markets comprise less than one percent of the total and are not listed here.

Table 9.1: The MSCI Global Investable Market Indexes (GIMI) classification

Developed markets:			Emerging markets:		
Americas	**Europe & Middle East**	**Pacific**	**Americas**	**Europe & Middle East**	**Pacific**
Canada	Austria	Australia	Brazil	Czech Republic	China
United States	Belgium	Hong Kong	Chile	Egypt	India
	Denmark	Japan	Columbia	Greece	Indonesia
	Finland	New Zealand	Mexico	Hungary	Korea
	France	Singapore	Peru	Kuwait	Malaysia
	Germany			Poland	Philippines
	Israel			Qatar	Taiwan
	Italy			Russia	Thailand
	Netherlands			Saudi Arabia	
	Norway			South Africa	
	Portugal			Turkey	
	Spain			United Arab Emirates	
	Sweden				
	Switzerland				
	United Kingdom				

Investors should utilize global allocation chiefly because different markets perform better at different times. This is not only due to variations in how assets behave relative to prevailing valuations, but also in response to changes in expectations of the economy and other geographic nuances.

Global allocation matters; next year's returns don't send invitations—you have to be there.

Further allocation benefits can be found by adding opportunistic "other equity" and global real estate.

- Other equity is any allocation an investor may make beyond the broad asset classes. Other equity may include investments in technology, energy, healthcare, and so on. Other equity is often a small opportunistic allocation of 5 percent of the portfolio and may be accomplished with an active manager or sector index fund.
- Global real estate is a separate asset class representing global real estate investment trusts (REITS). Typically, REITS hold apartment buildings, cell towers, data centers, hotels, medical facilities, offices, retail centers, warehouses, care homes, and self-storage.

STEP 2: DIVERSIFY BROADLY WITHIN MARKETS

Along with allocation, diversification is considered one of the most important decisions an investor can make. Diversification is created by holding different types of securities within a given market. Think of diversification as the depth of the market.

Diversification serves to capture the depth of the market

A second category that every public company belongs to is industry classification. The Global Industry Classification Standard (GICS) was developed by Morgan Stanley Capital International and S&P in 1999 to help global companies and investors compare and sort stocks. Every publicly traded company is evaluated quantitatively and qualitatively, and is assigned a single GICS classification. There are eleven classifications, as represented by their weight in their specific market. For example, Canada has a higher proportion of energy and financial sector companies than the US market does.

Table 9.2: Industry sector classifications, GICS weights, on December 31, 2021

Industry sector:	Canada Weight %	US Weight %	International developed Weight %	Emerging markets Weight %
Communication Services	4.75%	10.00%	4.50%	10.75%
Consumer discretionary	3.75%	12.25%	12.50%	13.50%
Consumer staples	3.5%	6.00%	10.25%	5.75%
Energy	14.50%	3.25%	3.25%	5.50%
Financials	33.50%	11.25%	17.00%	19.50%
Health care	0.75%	13.00%	12.75%	4.25%
Industrials	11.50%	8.00%	16.00%	5.00%
Information Technology	8.75%	28.25%	9.75%	22.75%
Materials	11.25%	2.75%	7.75%	8.75%
Real estate	3.00%	2.75%	2.75%	2.00%
Utilities	4.25%	2.50%	3.50%	2.25%

As shown in the table above, the industry weights are different, depending on the country. The Canadian equity market industry sector weightings are different than those of US and

International markets. This is further evidence of the benefits of global allocation to reduce portfolio risk and enhance returns.

Table 9.3: Example of recognizable companies and their respective industry sectors:

Communication Services	BCE / Meta / Google / Netflix / Walt Disney / Verizon / Shaw
Consumer Discretionary	Amazon / Carnival Corp / Tesla / Starbucks / Lululemon
Consumer staples	Walmart / Proctor and Gamble / Loblaws / Kraft / Costco
Energy	Suncor / Husky Energy / Chevron / Exxon / Kinder Morgan
Financials	Royal Bank / Visa / JP Morgan / PayPal / Berkshire Hathaway
Health care	Johnson & Johnson / Pfizer / Tilray / Medtronic / Teladoc Health
Industrials	Boeing / Caterpillar / 3M / General Electric / UPS / CN Railway
Information Technology	Shopify / Apple / Microsoft / Square / Adobe / Cisco
Materials	Barrick Gold / DuPont / Sherwin Williams / Rio Tinto
Real estate	Canadian Apartment / RioCan / American Tower / Public Storage
Utilities	Fortis / PG&N / Duke Energy / Hydro One / Emera

Diversification is a major factor in reducing risk and enhancing returns in a portfolio. Diversification strives to smooth the industry or stock specific risk events in a portfolio. The positive performance of some investments neutralizes the negative performance of others. Diversification works because industries and sectors are not highly correlated—that is, they respond differently, often in opposing ways, to market influences. For example, energy stocks are not perfectly correlated with technology stocks, and may move in the opposite direction, based on market news.

Allocation and diversification are the antidote to uncertainty.

STEP 3: FOCUS ON HIGHER EXPECTED RETURNS

VALUATION THEORY AND HIGHER EXPECTED RETURNS

Valuation theory provides a framework for the drivers of expected stock returns, linking expectations about a firm's future cash flows to its current value through a discount rate (or, equivalently, the expected return on the stock). Valuation theory is similar to the expected risk and return discussion for Uncle Bob and Uncle Steve (examples 3.2 and 3.3 / chapter 3). Using the valuation framework, we can expect small cap stocks to outperform large cap stocks, low-relative-price stocks to outperform high-relative-price stocks, and stocks with higher profitability to outperform low-profitability stocks. These differences are referred to as "dimensions" or "factors" of higher expected returns. These premiums are applicable to real portfolios because they are persistent over time, pervasive across markets, and cost-effective to capture. Consistent with valuation theory, the existence of these premiums has been documented in academic studies covering over forty countries and nine decades of stock data. There is an expanded explanation of these premiums in Appendices 2, 3, and 4.

Premiums or factors of expected higher returns that are applicable to building portfolios are:

1) **Size premium** = Small company returns—large company returns
   The size premium indicates that smaller companies have higher risk than large companies and therefore over time, have higher expected returns. In simple terms, investors, should they capture the size premium, would be compensated with returns greater than owning a basket of large companies.

2) **Value premium** = Value company returns—growth company returns
   The value premium indicates that value companies have higher risk than growth companies. Therefore, over time, value companies have a higher expected return. In simple terms, investors, should they capture the value premium, would be compensated with returns greater than if they owned a large basket of growth companies.

3) **Profitability premium** = High profitability company returns—low profitability returns
   A more recent premium, the profitability premium, was explained in a 2012 paper by Professor Robert Novy-Marx, entitled "The Other Side of Value: The Gross Profitability Premium." The paper not only provided investors with new insights into the cross section of stock returns, but it also helped explain Warren Buffett's superior performance—he invested in value companies with higher profitability metrics. Controlling for profitability dramatically increases the performance of value strategies, especially among the largest, most liquid stocks. Strategies based on gross profitability generate value-like average excess returns, even though they are growth strategies. Investors, should they capture the profitability premium, would be compensated with returns greater than a portfolio holding less profitable companies.

Exposure to multiple risk factors (dimensions of higher returns) can also add another layer of diversification to reduce risk and enhance return.

STEP 4: UTILIZE FINANCIAL SCIENCE

The broad term "science" probably brings to mind many different pictures: a textbook, white lab coats and microscopes, math equations scribbled on a chalkboard, the space station, periodic tables, and so on. Science is defined as the development of objective, consistent, documented systems of knowledge based on rigorous, systematic observations that lead to hypotheses that are then tested and refined.

Pigs can be launched into the air, but they don't fly

Science is evidence-based information that can be used in everyday life. In a noisy, social-media-driven world, we may get confused about what is fact, what is fiction, and who to believe. It can be comforting to fall back on decades of peer-reviewed research when evaluating all types of decisions. Financial science, also referred to as academic finance, is based on decades of rigorous, independent, peer-reviewed, time-tested research about how financial markets work and how market participants interpret financial information.

Markets feel chaotic; academia offers a sense of stability

The field of financial science and portfolio management has undergone a transformation in the last fifty years. The use of computers has made it possible for researchers to process large amounts of data to evaluate and understand sources of risks and returns. Computers have aided in the organization of data to enable new theories and models to be tested. An historical timeline of Nobel Prize laureates in Economics who have had a direct impact on portfolio management include:

1970	Paul Samuelson	Market Pricing Theory
1990	Harry Markowitz	Modern Portfolio Theory
1990	Merton Miller	Asset Pricing Risk
1990	William F. Sharpe	Capital Asset Pricing Model
1997	Robert Merton	Asset Pricing Risk
1997	Myron Scholes	Asset Pricing Risk
2002	Daniel Kahneman	Psychological insights into Economic Theory
2013	Eugene Fama	Empirical Analysis of Asset Prices
2013	Robert J. Shiller	Empirical Analysis of Asset Prices
2017	Richard Thaler	Behavioral Finance

Financial science and research topics discussed in this book include:

- Efficient market theory
- Market and security risk
- Valuation and dimensions of returns
- Portfolio construction, allocation, and diversification
- Behavioral finance
- Investor psychology

Financial science provides a valuable foundation of knowledge and wisdom to assist in the building and managing of portfolios. Financial science provides investment professionals with more education, more knowledge, and more understanding of how markets work. The immense value to everyday investors of the vast body of peer reviewed academic financial research should not be underestimated.

Investors watch, study, and invest in markets. The problem may be a lack of fundamental academic understanding of how markets actually work.

One of the fundamental concepts of asset pricing in publicly traded securities is the efficient market theory (EMT). The EMT is nothing more than the statement that security prices fully reflect all publicly available information. The value at which a transaction occurs, the market price, will reflect the buyers' and sellers' differing views of return and risk, at a point in time. New information, which arrives randomly, may affect the investor's perception of risks and returns. This may affect the market price in a positive or negative manner. The burden of active stock pickers is can they persistently predict the impact of this new information and buy the stocks that may go up and sell the stocks they think will go down? Fifty years of academic research suggest that active management, over time, does not add more value than passive index and asset class investing.

> "In academic finance, there are three to five ideas that survive every 20 years. In marketing and applied finance, there are 10 new products a week."
> —Eugene Fama

Finance and economics are also heavily influenced by behavioral psychology. The 2002 Nobel Prize in Economics was awarded to Daniel Kahneman for his work on the psychology of judgment and decision-making, and behavioral economics. Kahneman and others developed prospect theory (the pain of losing is greater than the joy of winning), and established a cognitive basis for common human errors that arise from heuristics and biases. Heuristics is defined as decision-making short cuts. A cognitive bias is a systematic error in thinking that occurs when people are processing and interpreting information in the world around them. Heuristics and biases affect the decisions and judgments of investors.

Behavioral economics is the meeting of finance and psychology

Financial science is the foundational knowledge that binds together the 7 Steps. Fundamental financial science is covered in Steps 1 to 3 (asset allocation, diversification, modern portfolio theory, and asset valuation). Behavioral financial science is covered in Steps 5 and 6 (judgment and decision-making). In the noisy and chaotic world of investing, financial science is critical to maintaining your sanity and keeping your portfolio strategy on track.

If your advisor is quoting Cathy Woods, Jim Cramer, or some other high-flying stock pickers, remind them that we have seen this story before. "Google: dot-com bubble 2000." The stock pickers that drive these bubbles come and go; the financial science just gets better.

Social media information is not likely to be evidence-based. Don't get your economic or investment advice from the university of YouTube or TikTok. Get it from someone who has a solid education, who understands and has studied peer-reviewed financial science.

> "The research suggests a surprising conclusion: to maximize predictive accuracy, final decisions should be left to formulas, especially in low-validity environments."
> —Daniel Kahneman

Academic evidence casts light on the challenges with traditional investment approaches, such as security selection and market prediction, and is guiding investors and advisors toward more research- / evidence-based investment strategies.

> "Modern finance is based primarily on scientific reasoning guided by theory, not subjectivity and speculation."
> —John "Mac" McQuown

The odds, over time, favor decision-making based on evidence-based financial science.

STEP 5: MANAGE STRATEGY RISK

Steps 5 and 6 are a reminder not to let behavioral issues derail Steps 1, 2, and 3. Investors can be emotional, and this emotion can be heightened during economic and market extremes. When markets are good—really good—investors' optimism can lead them to throw caution to the wind and take on too much risk. When markers are really bad, investors' pessimism may cause them to reduce risk at the wrong time. The "buy high, sell low" can cause grievous harm to investors' long-term results.

Don't let emotions and intuition drive your portfolio strategy off track

When markets are at their extremes is when investors should be most rational and logical. But we are human beings, and we feel fear and greed.

> "Even once we are aware of our biases, we must recognize that knowledge doesn't equal behavior. The solution lies in designing and adopting an investment process that is at least partially robust to behavioral decision-making errors."
> —James Montier

A portfolio is a collection of investments, or building blocks, adding up to 100 percent. Financial advisors are like portfolio coaches and risk managers. They determine portfolio strategy, asset allocation, what type and how much of any given investment, to put into a portfolio. Their influence and decision-making can have a significant impact on the success or failure of their clients' investment portfolios.

Strategy risk is the risk of not having a good strategy or not executing on a strategy. Investors may think they have a strategy when they do not. Just because there is a documented objective to achieve a given return does not imply they have a strategy to facilitate this objective.

Strategy risk is synonymous with bad management in a poorly run company

Advisors will often espouse what I call a "thin strategy." A thin strategy is bravado and hype, and thin on substance, structure, intelligence, and execution. The "I will work harder" or "I will make this work" might work as motivation for a child's soccer team but will have no material impact when managing the risks and returns in the global capital markets. Thin strategies are often exposed with evolving market cycles. Like many failed strategies, it will work until it doesn't. More than charisma and vison, investors must demand a well-designed, substance-based, and executable strategy.

Advisors, by the nature of the industry they are in, may be either too optimistic or too pessimistic. A confident, optimistic advisor can have strong emotions about where they think the market will go, or where they want the market to go next. A pessimistic, cautious advisor may appear to be trying to protect you from the next market downturn. Another type of advisor that may create strategy risk is the "Yes-man" advisor. "Yes-man" advisors tend to allow clients to rally around emotional, low probability choices, which increases non-compensating risks. An investor is best served by a more neutral advisor that utilizes a rules-based portfolio process and structure. A good investment strategy should be based on the client's long-term investment objectives and constraints and the nature of how markets work rather than on feelings about where the market will go next.

Strategy risk is synonymous with short-term thinking, lack of discipline, market timing, advisor indecisiveness, lack of systems to manage the variables that can be controlled, and decisions based on intuition, rather than evidence. A portfolio strategy should be based around a defined and proven structure. The lack of structure and an excessive number of individual investments can affect decision-making in rapidly changing markets. This results in additional decisions, more stress, and the added risk of making poorly informed decisions.

> "The best we can do is compromise: learn to recognize situations in which mistakes are likely and try harder to avoid significant mistakes when the stakes are high."
> —Daniel Kahneman

Daniel Kahneman notes that we too often rely on our intuition and routine thinking for big decisions, when we should actually slow down and become more analytical. In his book,

Thinking Fast and Slow, Kahneman helps us understand our thought processes using a framework of System 1 thinking and System 2 thinking. System 1 thinking operates automatically and quickly, "with little or no effort and no sense of voluntary control." System 2 thinking, on the other hand, allocates attention to effortful mental activities that demand it." Kahneman relates System 1 to fast thinking, and System 2 to slow thinking.

A rules-based, systematic portfolio process and structure, based on evidence-based information, will help manage impulsive thinking and reduce strategy and investment choice risk.

STEP 6: MANAGE INVESTMENT CHOICE RISK

Investment choice risk is essentially the risk of making a poor investment decision by choosing the wrong investment over the right investment. To be fair, picking the better investment from a basket of choices is not easy. Investors, however, are generally a confident bunch and can talk themselves into investing in almost anything. If strategy risk is about managing the portfolio process and structure, investment choice risk is the opportunity cost of making a bad investment choice. Some common investment choice risks can result from the following problems.

NOT UNDERSTANDING RISK

In 2021, a large, well-known Canadian investment mutual fund company created and marketed a Bitcoin fund and an Ethereum fund to investment advisors and retail investors. They marketed the funds, both in video and print, with two points:

1) The asset class has a low correlation with cash, stock, and bond markets
2) As the world becomes more digitalized, cryptocurrencies should become more popular

They then pointed out that compared to stocks, bonds, and cash, Bitcoin has been the best performer over the past one-, five-, and ten-year periods. Reading this or watching it on their YouTube video might lead you to believe it is a great investment.

This product is a classic investment choice risk because it's hard to understand the risks. I could be wrong—maybe this is a great investment. But I can't rationalize why an investment fund holding unregulated cryptocurrencies has any reason to be in a retirement portfolio, other than for its entertainment value. Furthermore, these investment products came about and were offered to their clients after the past returns of the crypto assets had been achieved. What are the odds of a new and disruptive type of investment, which has produced massive outperformance relative to other assets, continuing to see outperformance in the next decade? I don't know the answer because it has never occurred. There are no estimates for future expected risks and return. "It's a guess" is not an investment strategy.

DISREGARD FOR CHANGING RISKS

Another investment choice risk is when the investor or advisor has a disregard for changing risks. The problem is often caused by what psychologists refer to as the "recency effect" and "confirmation bias." The recency effect occurs when the investor only sees their recent returns and assumes a linear continuation of returns, without considering the merits of the future expected returns and risks. Confirmation bias may make this worse, as the investor only seeks out information that confirms what they want to believe. A good example of changing risks is when expected earnings growth rates start to decline, and investors confuse the concept of a good company and a good value. I will be examining this in Appendix 3 (under the "irony of growth"), when I examine the impacts of changing growth rates.

OVERCONFIDENCE BIAS

Overconfidence bias affects strategy risk and investment choice risk. The bias occurs when the advisor or investor overestimates their own abilities, believing they are smarter or more informed than they really are. Investors showing overconfidence may mistakenly equate information quantity with quality. They may feel overly confident if they have substantial amounts of information, even if its quality is poor. Overconfident investors tend to understate the risks and overstate the expected returns of an investment.

INDECISION RISK

Indecision risk is the inability to take action to manage risk. Buying an investment is easy. Deciding whether to hold it or sell it is the difficult part. The investor's inability to assess a given investment's risk and return because of either emotional attachment or indifference can add more unwanted risk.

Investors are often left holding a portfolio of what I referred to earlier as a "mixed bag" of mediocre investments. These investments may not provide compensating returns, relative to the risks they are accepting.

PRODUCT RATHER THAN SOLUTION

Investments should complement and add to the success of an overall portfolio. Be careful of advisors just selling you their company product or the product flavor of the day that may not be the best solution to add value to the portfolio.

CHASING PAST PERFORMANCE

Chasing past performance, as discussed in chapter 3, is the posterchild for investment choice risk. On the surface, investing should be simple. Place the current best performing investments in your portfolio. How hard can that be? You can certainly only put the recent best performers in your portfolio. In fact, a large part of the investment industry does just that. Unfortunately, investing is not as easy as picking the past year's winners. The best investments in one year, as research has shown, are not likely the best investments the next year. The markets are an ever-evolving pricing mechanism, and the past is seldom the future.

Investors need better self-awareness to counteract decision making bias

STEP 7: MANAGE COST AND TAXES

Investment management costs and taxes matter, whether you are managing an apartment building or a portfolio of investments. The costs of managing the investments will affect your net return.

Typical investment management costs include:

1) Trading costs:
   a. The direct cost to buy or sell an investment
   b. The spread between the bid and ask
2) Custodian fees
3) Management fees charged by the investment firm
4) Operating costs for a fund, including audits and reporting, and sales taxes on management fees
5) Trading costs (trading expense ratio [TER]) on funds
6) Trailer fees paid to the advisor (if applicable)
7) Management expense ratio (MER). This will total expenses 3 + 4 + 5, above, and may include 6, if applicable. The MER is the annual cost, as a percentage, of managing the investments
8) Advisory fees charged by investment advisor

Advisory fees pay for investment management, financial, tax, and estate planning. Like hiring a firm to manage your apartment building, you should hire the advisor to help you make informed decisions to improve your odds of long-term investment success. The decisions need to match your objectives, constraints, and risk tolerance.

The cost of any investing should be related to the value of the advice you receive

Investment costs can have a direct impact on investors' net returns. These costs need to be considered in the larger context of portfolio risk and return. Chasing the lowest cost investment option may reduce cost, but may increase overall investment risk. The increased risk of poor diversification or allocation, or poor choice of investment vehicles may reduce the odds of long-term investment success.

EXAMPLE 9.1: THE COST OF NO ADVICE

Advice may come at a cost, but no advice may cost you even more. Here is my version of a popular discount broker's advertisements on TV.

Two brothers, **Dave** and **Ray**, are taking about investments and moving away from their parent's brokerage firm to an online brokerage firm. Here is the dialogue:

Dave: "I bought shares in Super Cool Tech Co. at $135 last week with no commission. Today it's trading at $57—how can that happen?" **Ray**: "What was their valuation?" **Dave**: "Valuation? What's that?" **Ray**: "I learned that from Dad's guy."

The best approach is to evaluate all the investment costs through the lenses of "value for money." You don't buy the cheapest car, the cheapest vacation, or go to the cheapest school. You look to pay a price relative to the value of the good or service. Similar to going to a good school to learn from great educators, to improve your odds of a lifetime of better earnings power, the cost of investment advice should be evaluated relative to how well it may increase your odds of long-term investment success.

TAXES ON INVESTMENT INCOME:

Think of taxes like investing costs that will impact net return. Estimated combined (federal and provincial) tax rates for the top tax rate in British Columbia (March 2022):

- Capital gains   26.75%
- Dividends (eligible Canadian dividends)   36.54%
- Interest   53.50%
- Dividends (ineligible)   48.89%

Investors have several options to minimize taxes:

- Defer taxation using an RRSP
- Grow savings tax free in a TFSA
- Manage the timing of realized capital gains over many years
- Receive Canadian source eligible dividend in taxable accounts

With large taxable investment portfolios, the best way to minimize taxes is to use index and asset class funds:

- Due to less portfolio trading, index and asset class funds historically have lower capital gains distributions.
- Due to their lower costs, they can distribute more of their portfolio's dividend income.
- Investors requiring frequent cash flow can sell shares of the index or asset class funds to create homemade dividends of tax efficient capital gains.

SUMMARY OF THE 7 STEPS

Step 1: Global allocation (portfolio breadth) can reduce risk and enhance returns.

Step 2: Broad diversification (portfolio depth) can reduce risk and enhance returns.

Step 3: Exposure to multiple risk factors (dimensions of higher returns) can add another layer of diversification to reduce risk and enhance returns.

Step 4: Financial science, which is based on evidence-based information, can serve as a foundation to making better investment decisions and building better portfolios.

Step 5: Investors should always be conscious of the potential of strategy risk. Strategy risk means deviating from a proven strategy because of a distraction or confusion. Strategy based on Steps 1 to 4 is the process and structure that will capture the returns and manage the risks to improve the odds of a successful outcome.

Step 6: Investors should always be conscious of potential investment choice risk. One should understand the expected returns and risks of any new investment choice before investing.

Step 7: Understanding costs increases awareness of the value of investment advice.

TAKEAWAYS:

7 STEPS:

- is a rules-based, systematic portfolio process and structure that will facilitate better investment decision-making;
- will focus you on the variables you can control to better manage the variables you cannot control;
- will focus the investment approach on capturing returns and managing risk to improve the odds of long-term investment success;
- is an intelligent approach that will help you stay disciplined, manage the impact of never-ending investment noise, and contribute to a better investment experience.

Chapter 10

Evaluation Rubric

Better analysis can lead to better solutions

Which house should I buy? Where should I vacation next summer? What should I do with my life? When is the best time to put Grandma in a home? How should I invest my life savings over the next ten-plus years?

Picture yourself standing in front of a white board. You are tasked with the responsibility of determining a plan of action, based on certain criteria and objectives. You are examining and weighing all the evidence. You are evaluating all the pros and cons of different views and are considering any personal views. The goal is to chart an executable course of action that you believe, based on all the information you have at this time, will provide the best odds of long-term success.

> *"We have no control over outcomes, but we can control the process. Of course, outcomes matter, but by focusing our attention on process we maximize our chances of good outcomes."*
> —Michael Mauboussin

The success of a strategy will primarily be determined by the quality of your decisions and the framework with which to evaluate those decisions. The quality of your decisions will depend on what information is evidence based and what is opinion based. The successful achievement of your long-term goals will primarily be determined by improving the odds of many independent decision-making processes that add up over time.

7 STEPS TO A BETTER PORTFOLIO

Again, the 7 Steps are:

1) **Allocate across global capital markets**
2) **Diversify broadly within markets**

3) Focus on higher expected returns
4) Utilize financial science
5) Manage strategy risk
6) Manage investment choice risk
7) Manage costs and taxes

The three portfolio approaches (recap from chapter 8):

1) Portfolio of individual stocks (active investment management)
2) Portfolio of active mutual funds or managers (active investment management)
3) Portfolio of index and asset class funds (passive and semi-passive investment management

The evaluation rubric is a grading tool to evaluate each of the three portfolio approaches relative to the 7 Steps. The Steps all apply to variables investors control and should be considered when constructing and managing long-term pension-style portfolios. Individually, each Step is important. Collectively, the processes add up, improving the odds of long-term investment success.

Understanding and evaluating one's choices can help facilitate better decision-making

RUBRIC GRADING SYSTEM

Regardless of all the talk of "investors should to this, investors should do that," the end game is to capture return and manage risk to place the odds of long-term investment success in the investor's favor.

The grading will reflect the odds that a given portfolio approach can satisfy the objective of the specific Step. Upon evaluation of each of the portfolio approaches, relative to each Step, I will assign a grade as follows:

A   High odds of accomplishing the task
B   Moderate odds of accomplishing the task
C   Low odds of accomplishing the task

Disclaimer: The goal of this evaluation is to examine, from the perspective of the author, how a given portfolio approach can satisfy a given criteria. This evaluation is not to criticize any specific portfolio approach or investment choice. Investors, as expected, have diverse and different views of risk and return. Investors' decision-making processes will be influenced by experience, education, personality, emotions, and outside influences. We expect different perspectives on each side of a transaction, and without these differences, we would not have buyers and sellers.

STEP 1: ALLOCATE ACROSS GLOBAL CAPITAL MARKETS

Asset allocation has long been considered to have the greatest impact on a portfolio's long-term performance. A globally allocated portfolio can help capture a broad range of returns and deliver more reliable outcomes. Global allocation reduces portfolio risk and enhances long-term returns.

Evaluate each portfolio approach relative to its ability to accomplish the task of allocating the portfolio dollars across the global capital markets:

(i) <u>Portfolio of stocks and bonds</u>

It would be difficult to allocate a portfolio of individual stocks and bonds across the global capital markets in an effective manner. A small number of individual stocks and bonds would not be able to cover the breath of the global capital markets.

Grade: C

(ii) <u>Portfolio of active mutual funds</u>

A portfolio of active mutual funds would provide more coverage of the global markets than individual stocks could. However, active managers tend to hold concentrated positions in large cap companies. In addition, active managers focus on a select group of their favorite countries rather than allocating across all the countries in the Global Investable Market Indexes (GIMI).

Grade: B

(iii) **Portfolio of index and asset class funds**

Index and asset class funds are ideal portfolio building blocks for allocation across global capital markets. Index and asset class funds are designed to follow specific benchmarks and can cover broad asset classes in each market or geographic region.

Grade: A

Step 1	Portfolio of stocks and bonds	Portfolio of active mutual funds	Portfolio of index and asset class funds
Grade:	C	B	A

STEP 2: DIVERSIFY BROADLY WITHIN MARKETS

Along with allocation, diversification is considered one of the most important decisions investors can make. Diversification is a major factor in reducing specific stock and sector risks and enhancing return in a portfolio.

Evaluate each portfolio approach relative to its ability to accomplish the task of broadly diversifying the portfolio dollars within each given market:

(i) **Portfolio of stocks and bonds**

A portfolio of stocks and bonds may be able to diversify within a given market. For example, a Canadian portfolio of stocks may be able to invest across the eleven Global Industry Classification Standard (GICS) sectors of the Canadian equity market. However, limited to a small portfolio of stocks, this approach would not be able to cover the breath of more than one global market effectively.

Grade: C+

(ii) **Portfolio of active mutual funds**

Active managers tend to focus on their favorite sectors and may not get adequate coverage of all eleven Global Industry Classification Standard (GICS) sectors within a given market or markets. Owning several active funds will enable a broader reach across the global capital markets.

Grade: B+

(iii) **Portfolio of index and asset class funds**

Index and asset class funds are designed to be broadly diversified across the eleven Global Industry Classification Standard (GICS) sectors of a given market. As a result, they are ideal portfolio building blocks that can efficiently and effectively diversify the portfolio, within and across global markets.

Grade: A

Step 2	Portfolio of stocks and bonds	Portfolio of active mutual funds	Portfolio of index and asset class funds
Grade:	C+	B+	A

STEP 3: FOCUS ON HIGHER EXPECTED RETURNS

As noted in chapter 9 and Appendices 2, 3, and 4, academic research has pointed to systematic differences in expected returns across asset classes that are worth pursuing in portfolios. These differences or dimensions of higher expected returns premiums are:

- Value premium
- Small cap premium
- Profitability premium

Evaluate each portfolio approach relative to its ability to capture higher expected returns:

(i) **Portfolio of stocks and bonds**

A portfolio of individual stocks would not be able to focus effectively on any of the identified premiums. For example, it would be difficult to capture the value premium with a small number of investments in a portfolio.

Grade: C-

(ii) **Portfolio of active mutual funds**

Active funds, like a portfolio of stocks and bonds, do not have the breadth of holdings to capture the value, small cap, or profitability premiums effectively.

Grade: B-

(iii) **Portfolio of index and asset class funds**

Asset class funds holding hundreds or thousands of investments are specifically designed to focus on and capture the identified return premiums.

Grade: A

Step 3	Portfolio of stocks and bonds	Portfolio of active mutual funds	Portfolio of index and asset class funds
Grade:	C-	B-	A

STEP 4: UTILIZE FINANCIAL SCIENCE

Financial science provides a valuable foundation of knowledge and wisdom to assist in the building and managing of portfolios. Financial science provides investment professionals with more education, more knowledge, and better understanding of investment risk and return. The vast body of peer-reviewed, academic financial research can be of immense value to all investors.

Evaluate each portfolio approach relative to its ability to utilize financial science in the portfolio approach:

(i) **Portfolio of stocks and bonds**

Active stock pickers may cherry-pick the financial science they agree with, while ignoring the academic research they don't care to believe in. For example, stock pickers may utilize the momentum factor without understanding its limitations and risks.

Grade: C+

(ii) **Portfolio of active mutual funds**

Like active stock pickers, fund managers will target some academic research while ignoring the material that does not interest them. A recent example is the low market beta, more commonly known as the low volatility strategy. Focusing on low volatility or low market beta stocks is one way of reducing volatility in an equity portfolio. In recent decades, low market beta portfolios have enjoyed the additional benefit of market-like returns. However, investors should take caution before extrapolating this performance into the future. It is not obvious that stocks sorted on past market beta alone should be expected to consistently deliver above average returns. The math would expect portfolios targeting low market beta stocks to generally have lower expected returns than the market portfolio.

Grade: B

(iii) <u>Portfolio of index and asset class funds</u>

A global portfolio of index and asset class funds is built upon the foundation of financial science. Asset allocation, diversification, valuation theory, and behavioral finance are all considered in a portfolio of index and asset class funds.

Grade: A

Step 4	Portfolio of stocks and bonds	Portfolio of active mutual funds	Portfolio of index and asset class funds
Grade:	C+	B	A

STEP 5: MANAGE STRATEGY RISK

Steps 5 and 6 are a reminder not to let behavioral issues derail Steps 1 to 4. Investors are emotional and this emotion can be heightened during market extremes. When markets are good, really good, investors' optimism can cause them to throw caution to the wind and take on too much risk. When markers are really bad, investors' pessimism may cause them to reduce risk at the wrong time. The buy high and sell low can cause grievous harm to long-term investment results.

Financial advisors are like a portfolio's coach and risk manager. They determine portfolio strategy, asset allocation, and what type and how much of an investment to put into a portfolio. Through their influence and decision-making, they have a tremendous impact on the success or failure of their clients' investment portfolios. Strategy risk is the risk of not having a good advisor or a good strategy, or not executing on a strategy.

Evaluate each portfolio approach relative to its ability to manage strategy risk:

Evaluating strategy risk can be subjective. To simplify, I will suggest the question:

Looking at a given portfolio strategy during a major market move upwards or downwards, are you comfortable that you will stick with the current strategy?

(i) **Portfolio of stocks and bonds**

A strategy that holds a concentrated portfolio of individual stocks can, as result of constantly changing markets, increase investment decision-making. More decision-making requires more analysis of risk and can make the portfolio prone to more errors. It can also cause more stress for the investor. This can make maintaining a disciplined portfolio strategy difficult over rising and falling market cycles.

Grade: C+

(ii) **Portfolio of active mutual funds**

A portfolio of active mutual funds may experience two types of strategy risk:

1) Managers may experience style drift. A value manager may drift to become a growth manager, or an international manager may end up holding primarily US equities. This may create more risk than the original strategy intended.
2) Managing a portfolio of active funds can get complicated when managers underperform their benchmarks and peers. Firing underperforming managers and hiring outperforming money managers is a standard remedy for this approach. However, the future is equally uncertain for all investment managers. The stress of adding and removing managers at the wrong time can increase risk and reduce return.

Grade: B

(iii) **Portfolio of index and asset class funds**

A global portfolio of index and asset class funds reduces the number of portfolio decisions. Index and asset class funds seek to capture the return of their benchmark. They don't underperform or outperform, they just perform. An index fund is used as a portfolio building block to capture a given market. An asset class fund is a portfolio building block to capture the market plus value plus small cap plus profitability premium.

A portfolio of index and asset class funds can be easily rebalanced with evolving markets, which reduces strategy risk.

Grade: A

Step 5	Portfolio of stocks and bonds	Portfolio of active mutual funds	Portfolio of index and asset class funds
Grade:	C+	B	A

STEP 6: MANAGE INVESTMENT CHOICE RISK

Investment choice risk is the risk of making a poor investment decision by choosing the wrong investment, over the right investment.

Evaluate each portfolio approach relative to its ability to manage investment choice risk:

(i) <u>Portfolio of stocks and bonds</u>

A portfolio of individual stocks has a lot of moving parts, involving a lot of decision-making. The more decision-making, the higher the odds of making a mistake.

Grade: C

(ii) <u>Portfolio of active mutual funds</u>

There are endless active managers marketing their secret sauce of investment management. Selecting the right active manager for the right market at the right time may comprise more luck than skill.

Grade: B

(iii) <u>Portfolio of index and asset class funds</u>

Broad-based indices and asset class funds offer better diversification than active investment management, and follow a more transparent investment process, which means investors have a clearer idea of what they are getting. Index and asset class funds, designed to perform a specific task, are ideal portfolio building blocks.

Grade: A-

Step 6	Portfolio of stocks and bonds	Portfolio of active mutual funds	Portfolio of index and asset class funds
Grade:	C	B	A-

STEP 7: MANAGE COST AND TAXES

Investment management costs and taxes matter, whether you are managing an apartment building or a portfolio of investments. The costs and taxes of managing investments affect the net return to the investor.

Evaluate each portfolio approach relative to its ability to manage costs and taxes:

(i) <u>Portfolio of stocks and bonds</u>

There are two approaches to a portfolio of stocks:

- Buy and hold a concentrated portfolio of stocks over the long-term. Although this may be cost and tax effective, the trade-off is that this portfolio will be exposed to significant concentration risk.
- Actively trade individual stocks. The risks, trading costs, and taxes can be high.

Grade: B

(ii) <u>Portfolio of active mutual funds</u>

Active mutual funds will have higher management costs relative to index and asset class funds. Active investment funds may also be less tax efficient, due to their active investment transactions within the fund.

Grade: C

(iii) <u>Portfolio of index and asset class funds</u>

Index and asset class funds traditionally have lower investment management fees. In addition, the reduced trading activity will make them more tax efficient.

Grade: A-

Step 7	Portfolio of stocks and bonds	Portfolio of active mutual funds	Portfolio of index and asset class funds
Grade:	B	C	A-

RUBRIC SUMMARY

The 7 Steps focuses on variables investors can control to better manage the variables they cannot control. The rubric below summarizes the grades assigned for each of the three portfolio approaches relative to their ability to satisfy the objective of each of the 7 Steps.

	Portfolio of stocks and bonds	Portfolio of active mutual funds	Portfolio of index and asset class funds
Step 1: Allocate across global capital markets	C	B	A
Step 2: Diversify broadly within markets	C+	B+	A
Step 3: Focus on higher expected returns	C-	B-	A
Step 4: Utilize financial science	C+	B	A
Step 5: Manage strategy risk	C+	B	A
Step 6: Manage investment choice risk	C	B	A-
Step 7: Manage costs and taxes	B	C	A-

Each of the 7 Steps is an investment choice to consider when creating, executing, and maintaining a portfolio. Individually, the steps may seem inconsequential. However, combined, the Steps add up and can improve the investors' odds of long-term investment success.

WEIGHTED GRADING AVERAGE OF THE 7 STEPS:

	Portfolio of stocks and bonds	Portfolio of active mutual funds	Portfolio of index and asset class funds
Final grade:	C+	B-	A-

Based on evaluating the three portfolio approaches relative to the criteria of the 7 Steps, the prudent choice is to build a globally allocated, broadly diversified portfolio of index and asset class funds.

> "It's good to learn from your mistakes. It's better to learn from other people's mistakes."
> —Warren Buffett

We all want our strategy to function according to plan. This implies better managing the risk it won't.

TAKEAWAY:

- Always evaluate the pros, the cons, and the odds of alternative approaches to accomplishing a given goal.

Disclaimer: In a diverse world, everyone gets to choose their own medicine. Not everyone is going to agree with using these 7 Steps, or want to utilize a globally diverse portfolio of index and asset class funds.

7 Steps was never meant to be a criticism of other choices. As an author, I did my own grading of the approaches. Readers can come to their own conclusions. The purpose of *7 Steps* is to identify important portfolio issues and evaluate them relative to portfolio approaches. The goal of the evaluation is to determine which portfolio approach, relative to the 7 Steps, will provide the better odds of long-term investment success.

One can argue that a portfolio of stocks and bonds enables one to target their conviction of future expectations. There is no doubt a focused portfolio can experience impressive returns to compensate for the added risks. In addition, this type of portfolio can, over long time periods, be low cost and tax efficient.

Another can argue that selecting a portfolio of active managers enables one to vote for what they believe will be outperforming money managers in select markets. Active management can feel empowering when managers outperform.

Chapter 11

Sample Portfolio

A portfolio has a job to do!

The Sample Portfolio's designed like a personal pension plan. A personal pension-style portfolio is defined as a rules and evidence-based long-term portfolio approach. This type of portfolio is globally allocated and broadly diversified, similar to a large institutional pension plan. Investors choose this style of portfolio management to plan for future cash flow needs, and to increase the reliability and consistency of returns to support their long-range financial goals. The Sample Portfolio construction and management are guided by the 7 Steps to increase the odds of capturing the returns of the global capital market while managing the risks inherent in investing.

A portfolio equals 100

There is infinite information, opinions, and investment choices. However you have a finite portfolio allocation of 100 investment units or 100 percent. One should evaluate each investment unit through the lens of its intended role and relationship to other investments in the portfolio. The goal is to have the right allocation of the right investments to increase expected return and reduce expected risk in the portfolio. Portfolio managers can be considered a portfolio's general manager or coach. They design and manage the portfolio of investments to accomplish the goal of increasing the odds of a successful outcome.

Focus on increasing the odds of long-term investment success

MoneyBall, a book by Michael Lewis, is based on the true story of how the Oakland Athletics manager Billy Beane and his staff, reinvented, if not the game of baseball itself, then the game of baseball team management. "Moneyball" is about finding value where other teams don't see it; at the time, getting on base was an undervalued skill. The right combination of average and underappreciated players that have specific skills created an above average team.

> "The math works." "Over the course of a season, there's some predictability to baseball. When you play 162 games, you eliminate a lot of random outcomes. There's so much data that you can predict individual players' performances and also the odds that certain strategies will pay off."
> —Billy Beane

7 Steps to a Better Portfolio is like the MoneyBall of investing. The goal is to place the right combination of the right investments, with specific attributes, to shift the long-term odds of a successful outcome in your favor.

> "The secret of success is to do the common thing uncommonly well."
> —John D. Rockefeller Jr.

SAMPLE $1,000,000 PORTFOLIO

For our example, we will assume the following:

- Portfolio investment assets of $1,000,000 in a taxable account.
- The investor has a moderate risk tolerance.
- The investor will keep 17 percent in cash and low risk bonds to satisfy any possible cash flow needs.
- The portfolio is considered an additional asset to fund the investor's retirement needs in ten-plus years.

The Sample Portfolio is an example of a pension-style portfolio. The Sample Portfolio is not about entertainment and excitement. It is not about chasing hope or running from fear. It is not focused on yesterday's market returns or superstar investment managers. It is not about predicting the future. The portfolio process and structure are focused on capturing the global capital market returns in an efficient and effective manner while managing the inherent risks of investing. The process is about managing financial and emotional risk. The portfolio is about providing the long-term pension-style investor with better odds of a successful long-term outcome.

Disclaimer: The Sample Portfolio is a hypothetical pension-style portfolio for a given situation. The investor's investment objective, constraints, and risk tolerances need to be considered in the creation and management of their portfolio. Please discuss with an investment professional before making investment decisions.

Sample Portfolio

Allocation	Asset class	Value	# of countries	# of holdings	Range of allocation
0.50%	Cash	$5,000	1	1	0%–10%
16.50%	Global bonds	$165,000	20	1,400	10%–30%
21.00%	Canada	$210,000	1	440	15%–25%
24.00%	US	$230,000	1	2,400	20%–30%
16.00%	International	$160,000	21	3,760	14%–24%
9.00%	Emerging markets	$90,000	21	2,320	7%–12%
5.00%	Other	$50,000	1	50	0%–7%
8.00%	Global real estate	$90,000	18	390	6%–12%
100%	Total	$1,000,000			

Components

17%   GLOBAL BONDS AND CASH

Global bonds can enhance portfolio diversification by expanding available issuers, yield curves, and term structures. A global yield curve opportunity set provides flexibility, enabling the investor to extract potentially higher expected premiums. Global bonds include mortgages and loans. The portfolio would be hedged to the Canadian dollar to minimize currency risk.

70%   GLOBAL EQUITY

The global equity component will cover Canada, US, International developed and Emerging markets equity. The investment vehicles will target the broad indexes with factor tilts that target higher expected returns.

	Canada Equity	US Equity	International Equity	Emerging Markets Equity
Market (index) beta factor	Yes	Yes	Yes	Yes
Value factor	Yes	Yes	Yes	Yes
Small cap factor	Yes	Yes	Yes	Yes
Profitability factor	Yes	Yes	Yes	Yes

The Sample Portfolio uses funds offered by Dimensional Fund Advisors. Dimensional Fund Advisors (DFA) is the largest provider of broad market-based multifactor asset class funds. www.dimensional.com

5% OTHER EQUITY

Other equity is any allocation an investor may make beyond the broad asset classes. This may include technology, energy, precious metals, and financials. Other equity is often a small opportunistic allocation of 5 percent of the portfolio and may be accomplished with an active manager or sector index fund.

8% GLOBAL REAL ESTATE

Global real estate is a separate asset class, representing global real estate investment trusts (REITS). Typically, REITS hold apartment buildings, cell towers, data centers, hotels, medical facilities, offices, retail centers, warehouses, care homes, and self-storage.

Note: The sample portfolio will utilize the index and asset class funds best suited to accomplish the goal of capturing return and managing risk. The global bonds and other equity may involve the use of active management. For more information see the author's website or contact the author.

Many investors talk global allocation and broad diversification but walk concentration and focused risks!

7 Steps to a Better Portfolio

Checking against the 7 Steps:

1) **Allocate across global capital markets**
   The Sample Portfolio is allocated across the global capital markets.

2) **Diversify broadly with each market**
   The Sample Portfolio is primarily constructed with index and asset class funds to ensure broad diversification within each market.

3) **Focus on higher expected returns**
   The Sample Portfolio primarily utilizes index and asset class funds within the equity allocation to target and capture the higher expected return premiums:
   - Value premium
   - Small cap premium
   - Profitability premium

4) **Utilize financial science**

   Financial science, also referred to as academic finance, is the foundational knowledge that binds together the 7 Steps of the Sample Portfolio. Fundamental financial science covers Steps 1 to 3 (asset-allocation, diversification, modern portfolio theory, asset valuation, and so on). Behavioral financial science covers Steps 5 and 6 (judgment and decision-making). In the noisy and chaotic world of investing, understanding fundamental and behavioral finance will help keep the investor and the portfolio going in the right direction.

5) **Manage strategy risk**

   The Sample Portfolio is designed with a rules-based, systematic portfolio process and structure (Steps 1 to 3). Maintaining this disciplined portfolio process and structure will help reduce and manage any impulsive and emotional decisions and keep the portfolio on its intended course.

6) **Manage investment choice risk**

   The Sample Portfolio utilizes primarily broad-based index and asset class funds, which will minimize the traditional problem of investment choice risk.

7) **Manage costs and taxes**

   The taxes and investment management costs will be noticeably lower than for traditional active management approaches.

"The process of investing is like a game of amateur tennis, where the winner is the one who makes the fewest mistakes"
—Charles D Ellis

THE STEPS ADD UP TO IMPROVE THE ODDS OF LONG-TERM INVESTMENT SUCCESS

Global allocation and broad diversification are the antidotes to uncertainty

Investing is a game of decisions related to risk, returns, the odds, and time. Global allocation, broad diversification, targeting higher expected returns, utilizing sound investment vehicles, reducing costs and taxes, and managing yourself are key variables to long-term investment success. Good investing is about being on the right side of the odds with good strategies. You are tasked to make informed, evidence-based decisions and develop and apply good investment habits. A rules-based, systematic portfolio process and structure will help you capture future returns and manage risks and emotions to improve your odds of long-term investment success. The Sample Portfolio may appear to some, a simple portfolio. However, the brilliance behind it is what makes it all work.

"Simplicity is the ultimate sophistication."
—Leonardo da Vinci

TAKEAWAYS:

- Allocate globally and diversify broadly.
- Focus on higher expected returns:
    - Small Cap premium
    - Value premium
    - Profitability premium.
- Maintain the portfolio allocation and diversification through good and bad markets.
- Use the investment vehicle that best accomplishes the job of targeting the returns while managing the risk.

Chapter 12

Keep it Simple / Keep it Intelligent

Investing can be overwhelming!

Markets are going up and down. Stock symbols on your phone are green and red. The media talks about unemployment, pandemics, geopolitics, commodities, house prices, interest rates, and Elon Musk. Your partner is asking when you are going to retire. Your neighbour wants to discuss climate change. Your nephew wants you to invest in cryptocurrencies. Your golfing buddy warns of an oncoming market crash.

You're not sure what is happening, what it means, or what you should do.

Always something to worry about

New information and opinions either agree or disagree with our investment feelings. Information and new opinions can push and pull us between what we want to do versus what we should do. It is a psychological battle between what makes us feel fearful, greedy, and comfortable.

People are complex beings. Yet simple, intelligent, executable processes and habits can improve their odds of successful outcomes.

Searching for an answer

The solution is not an absolute. It is the relationship between you, your money, and your decisions related to risk, return, time, and odds. Like the solution to lose weight, be happier, and get more out of life, it comes down to attitude, discipline, behavior, and perspective.

FOUR INVESTMENT QUESTIONS

Ask yourself the four investment questions:

1) Why am I investing?
2) Where do returns come from?
3) What is risk?
4) How do I capture returns and manage risk?

Your answers to the questions require honesty. Why are you really investing? What is your investment horizon? What are your cash flow needs, and what is the time frame? Do you understand where returns come from and how they relate to risk? Do you understand investment risk? How have you reacted during past market declines? Do you have a willingness and ability to tolerate major down markets?

Do you know what you want? Do you have an executable plan?

The never-ending news may drive investors to do something, anything. As difficult as investing can be, it is not a good idea to try and force a round peg in a square hole. The idea that one can predictively guess market moves is a fantasy best left to fictional stories. Understanding, with evidence-based information, what has happened will help you understand why it happened. Understanding will help you develop a strategy to focus on the variables you can control.

Factors to consider:

- Long-term – rather than short-term
- Proactive policy driven approach – rather than forecast driven
- Pragmatic – rather than idealistic
- Rules-based systematic strategy – rather than indecisive
- Evidence-based research – rather than intuitive

Life has been a struggle for humans for thousands of years. We've created processes, structures, and habits to improve the odds of a better life. Investing is no different. We seek investment processes, structures, and habits to improve the odds of long-term investment success.

> "Life prepares you for investing and investing prepares you for life."
> —David Booth

UTILIZE AN INTELLIGENT PLAN THAT IS SIMPLE TO UNDERSTAND.

FOCUS ON WHAT YOU CAN CONTROL TO BETTER MANAGE WHAT YOU CANNOT.

Planning is like a road map. Planning is part of everyday life. You plan everything from your breakfast, your workday, and your weekends, to your kitchen renovation. Planning is an innate part of daily life. We are all looking for an intelligent executable plan that simplifies our life, not complicates it. Your decisions have consequences and impact on long-term outcomes. You look both ways before you cross the street—take the time to plan your investment strategy. Focus on risk management, investment process, and the variables you can control.

> "Process is the one aspect of investing that we can control. Yet all too often we focus on outcomes rather than process. Yet ironically, the best way of getting good outcomes is to follow a sound process."
> —James Montier

You and your portfolio are best served by using a rules-based, systematic investment process and structure to manage what you can control to better manage what you cannot. This approach will provide clarity, reduce the impact of investment noise, and facilitate better decision-making. This approach will keep you focused on your goal of capturing returns and managing risks. The approach will enhance consistency and reliability of returns to improve long-term financial planning. Investors need to appreciate that investing is a game of uncertainty, best managed with patience and intelligence, over a long period of time.

> "The essence of risk management lies in maximizing the areas where we have some control over the outcome while minimizing the areas where we have absolutely no control over the outcome and the linkage between effect and cause is hidden from us."
> —Peter Bernstein

The 7 Steps are not complicated concepts. Many, on their own, are universally accepted as foundations for a good portfolio approach. Combining them will help you navigate through the chaotic world of investment noise, opinions, investment choices, and investment questions. More informed investment decision-making improves the odds of a successful outcome.

7 Steps:

1) Allocate across global capital markets
2) Diversify broadly within markets
3) Focus on higher expected returns
4) Utilize financial science
5) Manage strategy risk
6) Manage investment choice risk
7) Manage costs and taxes

We are all stewards of our money. Make wise choices.

Investing is a game of decisions related to risk, return, odds, and time. Your goal is to utilize a systematic investment process and structure to manage yourself and your money to increase the odds of capturing return and managing risk over your investment horizon. I realize that for some, a pension-style investment approach may seem boring and lack excitement. I hope you now see that all the extra return generated from a disciplined structured portfolio approach can be spent on fun.

Good times, bad times

Markets are volatile and investing can be emotional. Investors need an intelligent, organized, executable portfolio process and structure that enables them to capture the good times, manage the bad times and narrow the range of outcomes in their favor.

> "Holding onto a sound policy through thick and thin is both extraordinarily difficult and extraordinarily important work. This is why investors can benefit from developing and sticking with sound investment policies and practices. The cost of infidelity to your own commitments can be very high."
> —Charles D. Ellis

A TALE OF TWO INVESTORS—REVISITED

In chapter 1, I introduced the two people sitting near you in the coffee shop; they were referred to as **Investor #1** and **Investor #2**. The investors do not know each other, but are identical in every way—same age, same net worth, same education, and most importantly, they have the same investment objectives and constraints.

Let's assume **Investor #1** follows the *7 Steps* and **Investor #2** does something else.

Investor #2 can predict and invest in anything at any time. Randomly he will make correct and incorrect investment decisions. It's is hard to know what **Investor #2** is going to do over months, years, and decades to come.

Investor #1 knows exactly what she is going to do. She is going to utilize a disciplined, rules-based, systematic portfolio process and structure. An intelligently designed framework, which incorporates evidence-based information, will facilitate better decision-making, and encourage better investing habits. **Her goal is simple; capture return and manage risk to improve her odds of long-term investment success.**

Investor #1 has the odds advantage

An odds advantage does not imply always achieving the win. It implies it is favored to win over long data periods. Investing is conducted in a very noisy arena and favorable and unfavorable randomness is expected. Over months and even years a random stock picking and market timing approach may achieve greater success than a globally allocated and broadly diversified portfolio of index and asset class funds. In fact, it would be expected that these types of portfolios, with the added risk, should randomly outperform. The problem is one will need to select the right investments, in the right markets, at the right time from the vast selection of options, to accomplish this outperformance. **Investor #1** has a long-term odds advantage by employing a disciplined rules-based systematic portfolio process and structure designed to capture the returns and manage the risks of the ever-evolving global capital markets.

IF I KNEW THEN WHAT I KNOW NOW

What I appreciate now, after years of education, and decades of client, investing, and teaching experience, is the importance of an intelligent, yet easily executable plan based on evidence-based information. Whether it's physical, mental, or financial health, help can be found in science and behavioral psychology. To increase the odds of a successful experience there is great deal of value in a rules-based, systematic process and structure that is built upon a framework of evidence-based information.

Be reflective and learn rather than fixated and stubborn

The act of making an investment does imply that you will attain the expected return. Uncertain outcomes are the very nature of investing. Understanding and respecting risk and return is fundamental to increasing the odds of long-term investment success.

Make fewer mistakes

There are no saints in investing. Fear, greed, and every emotion in between have at some time driven us to misinterpret information, misread odds, misunderstand risk. and make mistakes. Learning is not a straight line. Obstacles, opportunities, and emotions will affect how we perceive information, adapt to situations, acquire knowledge, and develop wisdom.

> "Investing is not nearly as difficult as it looks. Successful investing involves doing a few things right and avoiding serious mistakes."
> —John Bogle

The financial world is not falling apart; it can just feel that way sometimes

The investing journey is full of good luck, bad luck, and miscues. Investing can be kind and then brutally unkind. One moment, you're wealthier and feel confident, successful, and happy. A moment later, your wealth has declined, and you are gripped with fear, confusion, and a lack of trust in the financial system. You may believe your success is due to your predictions and the losses are the fault of others. Markets are ever-evolving pricing mechanisms that react to how investors perceive new information. New information is new, random, and never as predictable as we hope.

The meaning of life is finding purpose in the choices you make

Investing, like life, is full of endless choices, opinions, noise, and information. Developing a decision-making framework based on evidence-based information will help manage emotions and direct actions to solve the problems that require your attention. Making purposeful choices and understanding the consequences will increase the odds of a better outcome.

INVESTING IS ABOUT STRATEGY AND THE ODDS

Regardless of all the investing noise, information, and opinions, what matters over time is putting the odds in your favor. Long-term odds are everything. The odds are the reason we wear seatbelts and eat healthily. We inherently think of the odds in everyday life. The irony in investing is we may not consider the odds. Investors, affected by endless information, can become emotional short-term thinkers, rather than being rational mathematical thinkers. If we thought in a mathematical way, we may not have as much fun, but investing and portfolio management are not about fun. Portfolio management is about using a process and structure to manage our savings. It is about improving the odds of achieving a return to grow our savings over the next five, ten, and twenty-plus years. Investing is about capturing returns and managing risks. No one knows the future of returns of any asset class. We work with estimates. Working with these estimates, it would be prudent to structure our portfolio to focus on improving the odds of capturing the returns and managing the risks of the ever-evolving capital markets.

Finding the right strategy takes work. Sticking to it takes even more work.

When you attended school, you sacrificed thousands of hours of study to complete your education. You endure countless hours of exercise to stay in physical health. You have given up or avoided many types of foods over the years to maintain your health and weight. Investing is an exercise and sacrifice of time, money, and emotions. It's a cerebral effort to find the better portfolio strategy, create and manage it, and most importantly, stick with it over good and bad market cycles.

> "Life is really simple, but we insist on making it complicated."
> —Confucius

Intelligent solutions have a deeper connection upon reflection

Investors are best served with an intelligent rules-based, systematic investment plan, founded on evidence-based information. The plan should be easy to understand and simple to commit to. A grounded, steady-as-you-go plan will help you manage investment risks and capture returns. Most importantly, the plan will help you navigate the market noise in ever evolving up and down markets. Confidence in your strategy will keep you focused on maintaining a globally allocated and broadly diversified investment structure.

Odds are everything!
Managing the variables to improve the odds is everything else!

I wrote *7 Steps to a Better Portfolio* for you, the average long-term investor, to help identify, evaluate, and deal with critical investment issues. Whether you invest independently or alongside your advisor, *7 Steps* is an investment framework to help facilitate better decision-making along your investment journey, reduce investment stress, and improve your odds of long-term investment success.

You should utilize a substantive, intelligent rules-based portfolio process and structure as common practice and act on it with positive intent.

Luck and smarts. Luck is when you find it. Smarts is when you know what to do with it.

TAKEAWAYS:

- Think about how the four investment questions apply to you.
- Your investment strategy should be understandable, intelligent, executable, and maintainable.
- We are all stewards of our money. Make wise choices.
- Something is always happening. You don't have to manage it. You have to manage yourself and the variables you control.

Appendix 1

The Stock Picking Game

Investing is a bet on an expected outcome

The Stock Picking Game is a good example of how easy it is to make an investment choice. Investors, like many people, are good at having an opinion of a future outcome, whether or not they understand the facts, variables, or risks involved. It is human nature to voice a position on almost any topic. An investing opinion is not just guessing the outcome of tonight's hockey game. Investing involves returns and risks that can have a material impact on your long-term financial well-being.

Predicting the winners in the stock market, sports, and entertainment worlds, and even predicting the weather, is human nature. We can't help ourselves—we look at the past and present, make a rationalization, and predict a future outcome.

The rules of "The Stock Picking Game" are simple. Pick one stock for each of the ten years from the market of seven stocks. You can pick the same stock for ten years or pick a different stock each year.

After the final selection in year ten, we will calculate the compounded average return of your selected investments over the ten years. The return is calculated using the standard geometric return. The geometric average return is a way to calculate the average rate of return on an investment that is compounded over multiple periods. The formula and examples of how it works are at the end of this appendix. You can also enter your selections and calculate your returns using the website at www.7stepstoabetterportfolio.com

Each stock is assigned a letter of the alphabet as its trading symbol. There are seven companies, as represented by the following stock symbols:

Stock   A
Stock   B
Stock   C
Stock   D
Stock   E
Stock   F
Stock   G

Each company is of similar financial size, based on assets and revenues. Let's assume each company stock price is currently $100. All of the companies are covered by investment analysts, and all currently have a buy rating and a one-year target of $110. The companies do not, and are not expected to, pay any dividends over the next ten years.

After picking a company in year one, it is assumed that if you pick a different stock in year two, it means that you sold the year one stock and no longer own it. To keep the game simple, we will ignore trading costs and taxes.

OBJECTIVE OF THE GAME:

1) Evaluate whether you can pick the right stocks over a ten-year period and outperform the average return of all seven stocks over that same time frame.
2) Compare your ten-year stock picking returns with the average returns of your friends and family.

Markets are an efficient real-time, information-processing mechanism

Disclaimer: Picking stocks without qualitative and quantitative research may not be realistic. However, in a relatively efficient market the return of any given stock is random and unpredictable. In that sense, the randomness of the stock picking game may not be very different than picking real stocks.

YEAR ONE SELECTION

Here are the past three years' returns for stocks A to G.

Using the past three years' data, your favorite letter, and any gut feelings select your first stock.

Please pick one of the stocks as your year one investment choice:

Pick	1	Prior 3 years	Prior 2 years	Prior 1 year	Year one
Stock	A	-8%	10%	-10%	**A**
Stock	B	30%	5%	0%	**B**
Stock	C	-8%	15%	7%	**C**
Stock	D	-10%	8%	12%	**D**
Stock	E	-5%	28%	-10%	**E**
Stock	F	24%	12%	9%	**F**
Stock	G	10%	22%	-5%	**G**

YEAR TWO SELECTION

The results for year one are shown below.

With year one completed, you can elect to hold onto your current stock or select another stock.

Please pick one of the stocks as your year two investment choice:

Pick	2	Prior 3 years	Prior 2 years	Prior 1 year	**Year one**	**Year two**
Stock	A	-8%	10%	-10%	-10%	**A**
Stock	B	30%	5%	0%	30%	**B**
Stock	C	-8%	15%	7%	25%	**C**
Stock	D	-10%	8%	12%	32%	**D**
Stock	E	-5%	28%	-10%	-5%	**E**
Stock	F	24%	12%	9%	3%	**F**
Stock	G	10%	22%	-5%	2%	**G**

YEAR THREE SELECTION

The results for year two are shown below.

With year two completed, you can elect to hold onto your current stock or select another stock.

Please pick one of the stocks as your year three investment choice:

Pick	3	Prior 3 years	Prior 2 years	Prior 1 year	**Year one**	**Year two**	**Year three**
Stock	A	-8%	10%	-10%	-10%	10%	**A**
Stock	B	30%	5%	0%	30%	-15%	**B**
Stock	C	-8%	15%	7%	25%	30%	**C**
Stock	D	-10%	8%	12%	32%	0%	**D**
Stock	E	-5%	28%	-10%	-5%	28%	**E**
Stock	F	24%	12%	9%	3%	6%	**F**
Stock	G	10%	22%	-5%	2%	22%	**G**

YEAR FOUR SELECTION

The results for year three are shown below.

With year three completed, you can elect to hold onto your current stock or select another stock.

Please pick one of the stocks as your year four investment choice:

Pick	4	Prior 3 years	Prior 2 years	Prior 1 year	**Year one**	**Year two**	**Year three**	**Year four**
Stock	A	-8%	10%	-10%	-10%	10%	-10%	A
Stock	B	30%	5%	0%	30%	-15%	0%	B
Stock	C	-8%	15%	7%	25%	30%	20%	C
Stock	D	-10%	8%	12%	32%	0%	-15%	D
Stock	E	-5%	28%	-10%	-5%	28%	-10%	E
Stock	F	24%	12%	9%	3%	6%	9%	F
Stock	G	10%	22%	-5%	2%	22%	-5%	G

YEAR FIVE SELECTION

The results for year four are shown below.

With year four completed, you can elect to hold onto your current stock or select another stock.

Please pick one of the stocks as your year five investment choice:

Pick 5		Prior 3 years	Prior 2 years	Prior 1 year	**Year one**	**Year two**	**Year three**	**Year four**	**Year five**
Stock	A	-8%	10%	-10%	-10%	10%	-10%	30%	**A**
Stock	B	30%	5%	0%	30%	-15%	0%	10%	**B**
Stock	C	-8%	15%	7%	25%	30%	20%	0%	**C**
Stock	D	-10%	8%	12%	32%	0%	-15%	45%	**D**
Stock	E	-5%	28%	-10%	-5%	28%	-10%	10%	**E**
Stock	F	24%	12%	9%	3%	6%	9%	-15%	**F**
Stock	G	10%	22%	-5%	2%	22%	-5%	10%	**G**

YEAR SIX SELECTION

The results for year five are shown below.

With year five completed, you can elect to hold onto your current stock or select another stock.

Please pick one of the stocks as your year six investment choice:

Pick	6	Year one	Year two	Year three	Year four	Year five	Year six
Stock	A	-10%	10%	-10%	30%	5%	**A**
Stock	B	30%	-15%	0%	10%	21%	**B**
Stock	C	25%	30%	20%	0%	2%	**C**
Stock	D	32%	0%	-15%	45%	44%	**D**
Stock	E	-5%	28%	-10%	10%	0%	**E**
Stock	F	3%	6%	9%	-15%	3%	**F**
Stock	G	2%	22%	-5%	10%	5%	**G**

YEAR SEVEN SELECTION

The results for year six are shown below.

With year six completed, you can elect to hold onto your current stock or select another stock.

Please pick one of the stocks as your year seven investment choice:

Pick	7	**Year one**	**Year two**	**Year three**	**Year four**	**Year five**	**Year six**	**Year seven**
Stock	A	-10%	10%	-10%	30%	5%	8%	**A**
Stock	B	30%	-15%	0%	10%	21%	20%	**B**
Stock	C	25%	30%	20%	0%	2%	35%	**C**
Stock	D	32%	0%	-15%	45%	44%	25%	**D**
Stock	E	-5%	28%	-10%	10%	0%	20%	**E**
Stock	F	3%	6%	9%	-15%	3%	-8%	**F**
Stock	G	2%	22%	-5%	10%	5%	20%	**G**

YEAR EIGHT SELECTION

The results for year seven are shown below.

With year seven completed, you can elect to hold onto your current stock or select another stock.

Please pick one of the stocks as your year eight investment choice:

Pick	8	Year one	Year two	Year three	Year four	Year five	Year six	Year seven	Year eight
Stock	A	-10%	10%	-10%	30%	5%	8%	-5%	A
Stock	B	30%	-15%	0%	10%	21%	20%	15%	B
Stock	C	25%	30%	20%	0%	2%	35%	15%	C
Stock	D	32%	0%	-15%	45%	44%	25%	12%	D
Stock	E	-5%	28%	-10%	10%	0%	20%	5%	E
Stock	F	3%	6%	9%	-15%	3%	-8%	3%	F
Stock	G	2%	22%	-5%	10%	5%	20%	5%	G

YEAR NINE SELECTION

The results for year eight are shown below.

With year eight completed, you can elect to hold onto your current stock or select another stock.

Please pick one of the stocks as your year nine investment choice:

Pick	9	Year one	Year two	Year three	Year four	Year five	Year six	Year seven	Year eight	Year nine
Stock	A	-10%	10%	-10%	30%	5%	8%	-5%	10%	A
Stock	B	30%	-15%	0%	10%	21%	20%	15%	5%	B
Stock	C	25%	30%	20%	0%	2%	35%	15%	14%	C
Stock	D	32%	0%	-15%	45%	44%	25%	12%	5%	D
Stock	E	-5%	28%	-10%	10%	0%	20%	5%	10%	E
Stock	F	3%	6%	9%	-15%	3%	-8%	3%	-2%	F
Stock	G	2%	22%	-5%	10%	5%	20%	5%	10%	G

YEAR TEN SELECTION

The results for year nine are shown below.

With year nine completed, you can elect to hold onto your current stock or select another stock.

Please pick one of the stocks as your year 10 investment choice:

Pick	10	Year one	Year two	Year three	Year four	Year five	Year six	Year seven	Year eight	Year nine	Year ten
Stock	A	-10%	10%	-10%	30%	5%	8%	-5%	10%	20%	**A**
Stock	B	30%	-15%	0%	10%	21%	20%	15%	5%	-15%	**B**
Stock	C	25%	30%	20%	0%	2%	35%	15%	14%	-25%	**C**
Stock	D	32%	0%	-15%	45%	44%	25%	12%	5%	8%	**D**
Stock	E	-5%	28%	-10%	10%	0%	20%	5%	10%	10%	**E**
Stock	F	3%	6%	9%	-15%	3%	-8%	3%	-2%	10%	**F**
Stock	G	2%	22%	-5%	10%	5%	20%	5%	10%	15%	**G**

STOCK PICKING GAME—CONCLUSION

The stock picking game is over!

Below are the returns for each of the past ten years:

Summary		Year One	Year Two	Year Three	Year Four	Year Five	Year Six	Year Seven	Year Eight	Year Nine	Year Ten
Stock	A	-10%	10%	-10%	30%	5%	8%	-5%	10%	20%	10%
Stock	B	30%	-15%	0%	10%	21%	20%	15%	5%	-15%	10%
Stock	C	25%	30%	20%	0%	2%	35%	15%	14%	-25%	0%
Stock	D	32%	0%	-15%	45%	44%	25%	12%	5%	8%	9%
Stock	E	-5%	28%	-10%	10%	0%	20%	5%	10%	10%	-15%
Stock	F	3%	6%	9%	-15%	3%	-8%	3%	-2%	10%	9%
Stock	G	2%	22%	-5%	10%	5%	20%	5%	10%	15%	-15%
		11%	11.57%	-1.57%	12.86%	11.43%	17.14%	7.14%	7.43%	3.29%	1.14%

The geometric average (actual compounding of cash flow) of the portfolio is 8.00%

100	11%	11.57%	-1.57%	12.86%	11.43%	17.14%	7.14%	7.43%	3.29%	1.14%	8.00%
100	111	124	122	138	153	180	192	207	213	216	8.00%

The geometric average uses the compounding of the cash flows to calculate portfolio returns

To calculate your portfolio's returns:

OPTION #1

Use the website and enter in your selected years' returns:

www.7stepstoabetterportfolio.com

OPTION #2

Use a BA II business calculator to calculate the returns:

An example of how to calculate the geometric return for the annual data for Company G is shown here.

100	2%	22%	-5%	10%	5%	20%	5%	10%	15%	-15%	6.34%
100	102	124	118	130	137	164	172	189	218	185	6.34%

Using a BA II Calculator

= ((1+.02) *(1+.22) *(1-.05) *(1+.10) *(1+.05) *(1+.20) *(1+.05) *(1+.10) *(1+.15) *(1-.15)) ^ 1/10 – 1

= (1.02 x1.22 x.95 x1.10 x1.05 x1.20 x1.05 x1.10 x1.15 x.85) ^ 1/10 – 1 = 6.344%

The ^ is the yx button on the BA II Calculator

Appendix 2

Size Premium

Investing risk is inseparable from return

The size premium is the historical tendency for the stocks of firms with smaller market capitalizations to outperform the stocks of firms with larger market capitalizations.

Size premium = Small company returns—large company returns

The size premium is extra compensation required by investors to invest in smaller, riskier companies versus larger, less risky companies. Large companies appear more attractive and are perceived to be less risky, relative to small companies. Investors are willing to pay higher stock prices for the higher expected safety.

APPENDIX EXAMPLE 2.1: SMALLER COMPANIES ARE PERCEIVED TO BE RISKIER

Let us assume there are two companies that would like you to invest $50,000 in their common shares. With common shares, you are a fractional owner of the company. With ownership, you would participate in any growth of the company and any dividends that they could, or may choose to, pay shareholders. With ownership, if the business were to fail, you could lose your total investment.

Large Co is a large manufacturing company. Your perception is that the company is financially stable, is under the guidance of good management, and has a broad base of customers. You would consider investing if you could expect a return of 10 percent.

Small Co is a smaller manufacturing company. While the small company is financially stable, and management appears to be good, your perception is that this company is riskier than the large company. You would consider investing only if you could expect a return of 15 percent.

In simple terms, investing in Large Co would appear to be a lower risk proposition. If however, you invest in Small Co, your payoff, in the form of a higher return, is compensation for accepting more risk. You have determined the expected return you would accept, based on the risks you perceive. You, as the investor, require a return of 10 percent to invest in Large Co and a return of 15 percent to invest in Small Co. This is an important concept in understanding risk, return, and asset pricing.

THERE ARE SEVERAL REASONS SMALL COMPANIES ARE PERCEIVED TO BE RISKIER:

1) Potential competition issues. It is easier to enter the market and compete with small companies, while larger companies have resources to mitigate competitive challenges.
2) Economic issues and concerns. Larger companies can better cope with economic downturns than small companies.
3) Limited access to capital. Small companies can find it difficult to obtain funding, while larger companies typically have more options for funding.
4) Management depth concerns. Large companies may not have key employee concerns in the same way that smaller companies do.
5) Customer concentration and product concentration risk. Small companies are typically not as diversified in product offerings and are often reliant on a small group of customers.
6) Liquidity concerns and lack of market coverage. Small companies do not enjoy the same level of analyst coverage, and small company stock is typically less liquid than larger companies.

Risk and expected return, as discussed in chapter 3, are inseparable. When you choose to invest your money, you the investor, evaluate your return expectations relative to risk. As in the Uncle Bob and Uncle Steve story (example 3.2 and 3.3 / chapter 3) you may have similar views on risk and expected returns with an investment in a large versus small company.

The higher risk of investing in small stocks versus large stocks should translate to a higher return. As noted in Appendix exhibit 2.1, the expectations are proven correct. Small company returns have, historically, been greater than large company returns.

The caveat with the size premium is that to capture it effectively investors need to:

- Invest over long periods of time
- Invest across hundreds, if not thousands, of companies
- Understand that the size premiums can materialize quickly, and you want to be properly positioned to capture the returns when they show up

APPENDIX EXHIBIT 2.1: HISTORICAL SIZE PREMIUMS

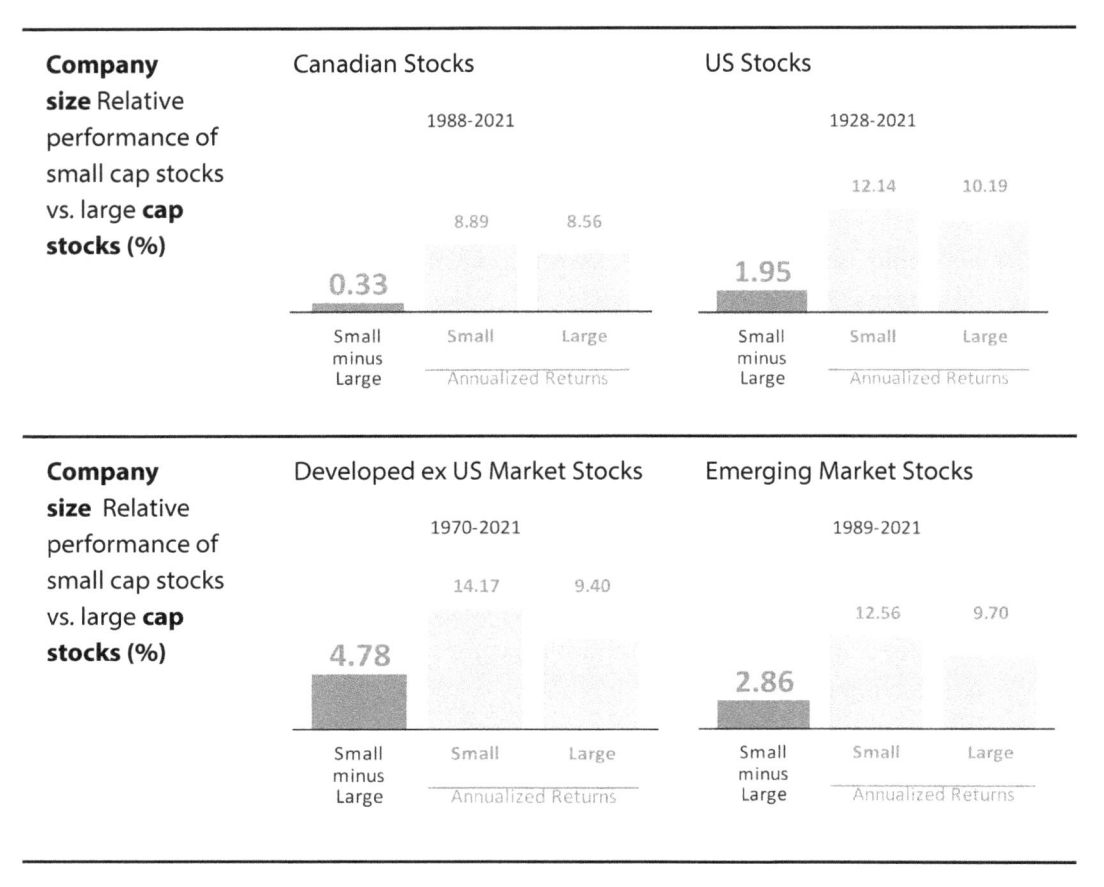

Company size Relative performance of small cap stocks vs. large **cap stocks (%)**

Canadian Stocks (1988-2021):
- Small minus Large: 0.33
- Small Annualized Returns: 8.89
- Large Annualized Returns: 8.56

US Stocks (1928-2021):
- Small minus Large: 1.95
- Small Annualized Returns: 12.14
- Large Annualized Returns: 10.19

Company size Relative performance of small cap stocks vs. large **cap stocks (%)**

Developed ex US Market Stocks (1970-2021):
- Small minus Large: 4.78
- Small Annualized Returns: 14.17
- Large Annualized Returns: 9.40

Emerging Market Stocks (1989-2021):
- Small minus Large: 2.86
- Small Annualized Returns: 12.56
- Large Annualized Returns: 9.70

Information provided by Dimensional Fund Advisors LP.

Past performance is no guarantee of future results. Actual returns may be lower.
All returns are in USD, except Canadian stock returns, which are in CAD. MSCI indices are gross div. **Indices are not available for direct investment. Index returns are not representative of actual portfolios and do not reflect costs and fees associated with an actual investment.** For Canadian stocks, indices are used as follows. Small Cap minus Large Cap: Dimensional Canada Small Index minus the S&P/TSX Composite Index. For US stocks, indices are used as follows. Small Cap minus Large Cap: Dimensional US Small Cap Index minus the S&P 500 Index For developed ex US stocks, indices are used as follows. Small Cap minus Large Cap: Dimensional International Small Cap Index minus the MSCI World ex USA Index. For Emerging Markets stocks, indices are used as follows. Small Cap minus Large Cap: Dimensional Emerging Markets Small Cap Index minus MSCI Emerging Markets Index S&P and S&P/TSX data © 2022 S&P Dow Jones Indices LLC, a division of S&P Global. All rights reserved. MSCI data © MSCI 2022, all rights reserved.

Appendix 3

Value Premium

Investing risk is inseparable from return

The value premium refers to the greater return, over time, of value stocks over growth stocks. Like the size premium, the value premium is based on how investors perceive and price risk.

Value premium = Value company returns—growth company returns

The value premium is the extra compensation required by investors that invest in less attractive value companies versus more attractive growth companies. Growth companies appear more attractive and are perceived to be less risky, relative to value stocks. Investors are willing to pay higher stock prices for the higher expected growth rates.

APPENDIX EXAMPLE 3.1: VALUE COMPANIES ARE PERCEIVED TO BE RISKIER

Let us assume there are two companies that would like you to invest $50,000 in their common shares. With common shares you are a fractional owner of the company. With ownership you would participate in any growth of the company and any dividends that they could, or may choose to, pay shareholders. With ownership, if the business were to fail you could lose your total investment.

Growth Co has, in recent years, experienced an increased revenue and earnings growth rate that is expected to continue for the foreseeable future. This growth rate is attributable to what is perceived to be excellent management, executing a solid business plan. It appears to be an exciting business with excellent business prospects. You are willing to pay a higher price per share, relative to current earnings, as you assume this is a lower risk investment. This perceived risk translates into a required or expected return of 10 percent.

Value Co has experienced some recent business setbacks that have affected earnings growth. The poor business performance is attributed to what is perceived as poor management and business decisions. You are not willing to pay a high price per share, relative to earnings, as you assume this is a riskier investment. This perceived risk translates into a required or expected return of 15 percent.

In simple terms, investing in Growth Co would appear to be a lower risk proposition. If however, you invest in Value Co, your payoff, in the form of a higher return, is compensation for accepting more risk. You have determined the expected return you would accept, based on the risks you perceive. You, as the investor, require a return of 10 percent to invest in Growth Co and a return of 15 percent to invest in Value Co. This is an important concept in understanding risk, return, and asset pricing.

The value versus growth premium is also referred to as the relative price premium. Growth stocks are historically perceived to be better investments, which causes investors to bid up the price relative to traditional valuation metrics like price to book, price to sales, and price to earnings. Value companies, lacking any positive developments, find their share prices at low levels relative to book value, earnings, and cash flow per share. Value investing may also refer to owning mature slower-growing businesses that may have higher dividend payouts.

THERE ARE SEVERAL REASONS THAT VALUE COMPANIES ARE PERCEIVED TO BE RISKIER:

1) Value companies are often "turnaround" business stories, and they may appear to have an uphill road to remain competitive with their peers.
2) Management may have lost some key personnel.
3) Business strategies are not working as expected.
4) Value companies may sit in out-of-favor sectors and trade at a price multiple much lower than seen in the broad markets. US financial institutions in 2009, and oil and gas stocks in 2020, are good examples.
5) Value companies, with low share prices and poor credit rating, will have higher cost of capital.
6) Value companies may experience higher employee turnover and have a harder time attracting highly qualified employees.
7) Existing customers and potential new customers may be concerned by the perception of a faltering business.
8) Value companies may be in highly competitive markets that are experiencing low growth rates.

Value investing means taking more risk and it requires patience. Perhaps the best-known value investor is Berkshire Hathaway leader, Warren Buffett.

Risk and expected return, as discussed in chapter 3, are inseparable. When you choose to invest your money, you the investor, evaluate your return expectations relative to risk. As in the Uncle Bob and Uncle Steve story (example 3.2 and 3.3 / chapter 3) you may have similar views on risk and expected returns with an investment in growth versus value companies.

The higher risk of investing in value stocks versus growth stocks should translate to higher returns. As noted in Appendix exhibit 3.1, the expectations are proven correct. Value company returns have historically been greater than growth company returns.

APPENDIX EXHIBIT 3.1: HISTORICAL VALUE (PRICE) PREMIUMS

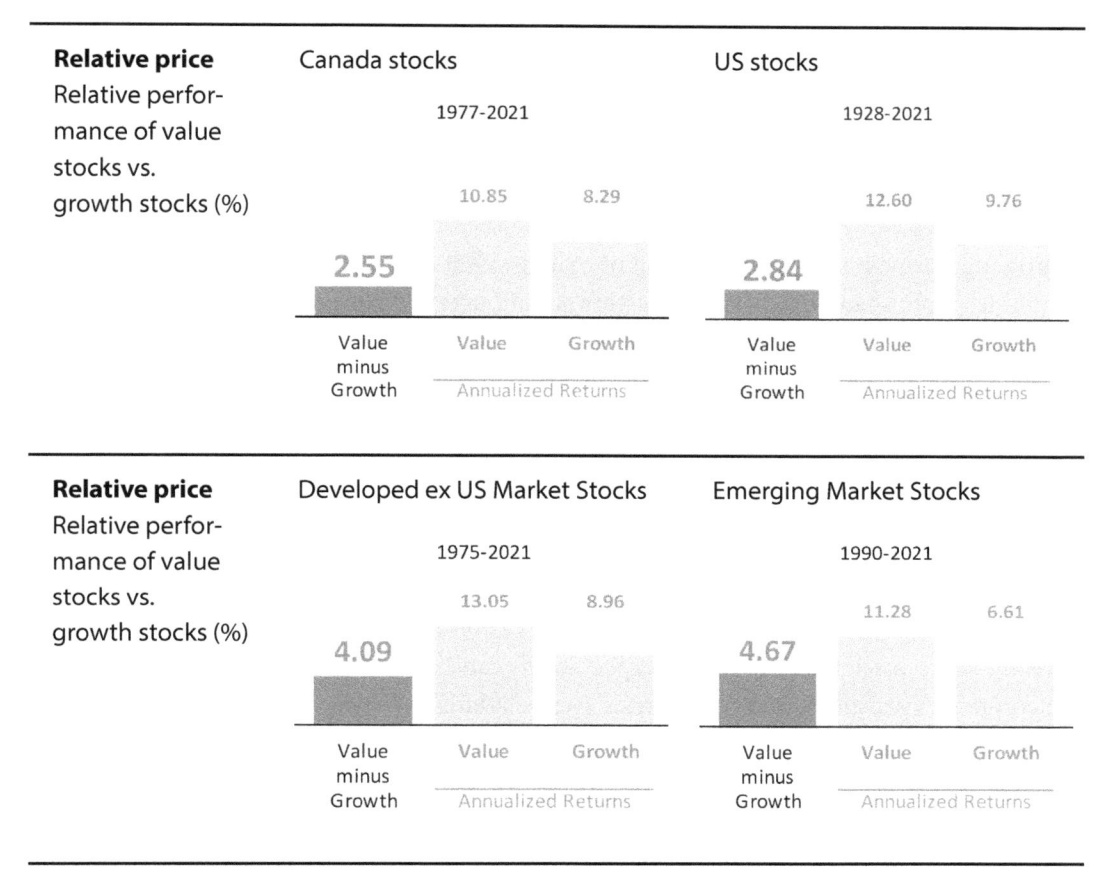

Relative price
Relative performance of value stocks vs. growth stocks (%)

Canada stocks — 1977-2021
- Value minus Growth: 2.55
- Value Annualized Returns: 10.85
- Growth Annualized Returns: 8.29

US stocks — 1928-2021
- Value minus Growth: 2.84
- Value Annualized Returns: 12.60
- Growth Annualized Returns: 9.76

Relative price
Relative performance of value stocks vs. growth stocks (%)

Developed ex US Market Stocks — 1975-2021
- Value minus Growth: 4.09
- Value Annualized Returns: 13.05
- Growth Annualized Returns: 8.96

Emerging Market Stocks — 1990-2021
- Value minus Growth: 4.67
- Value Annualized Returns: 11.28
- Growth Annualized Returns: 6.61

Information provided by Dimensional Fund Advisors LP.

Past performance is no guarantee of future results. Actual returns may be lower.
All returns are in USD, except Canadian stock returns, which are in CAD. MSCI indices are gross div. **Indices are not available for direct investment. Index returns are not representative of actual portfolios and do not reflect costs and fees associated with an actual investment.** For Canadian stocks, indices are used as follows. Value minus Growth: Fama/French Canada Value Index minus the Fama/French Canada Growth Index. For US stocks, indices are used as follows. Value minus Growth: Fama/French US Value Research Index minus the Fama/French US Growth Research Index For developed ex US stocks, indices are used as follows. Value minus Growth: Fama/French International Value Index minus the Fama/French International Growth Index. For Emerging Markets stocks, indices are used as follows. Value minus Growth: Fama/French Emerging Markets Value Index minus Fama/French Emerging Markets Growth Index. S&P and S&P/TSX data © 2022 S&P Dow Jones Indices LLC, a division of S&P Global. All rights reserved. MSCI data © MSCI 2022, all rights reserved.

The caveat with the value premium is that to capture it effectively investors need to:
- Invest over long periods of time;
- Invest across hundreds, if not thousands, of companies;
- Understand that the value premiums can materialize quickly, and you want to be properly positioned to capture the returns when they show up.

The irony of growth

A growing business is the embodiment of management success, positive change, and innovation. It would seem logical that investors should over-weight growth companies in their portfolios. However, given that the market is relatively efficient at pricing assets based on all current news, the current price of the growth company shares will undoubtably already reflect all the optimism of future growth.

The irony of growth is that once a company is deemed a notable growth company, the best years of its growth may be in the past. Competition, defecting talent, substitute products and changing consumer demands can impact future growth rates. However when investors see a company or sector of the market experiencing rapid sales and earnings growth, investors may extrapolate this data as an expectation of continued linear growth into the future. A rising share price based on these expectations can create a false sense of confidence in the company's prospects and future price appreciation. The rising share price may instill a false sense of confidence in the investor that a given company is a less risky investment. The problem is that growth expectations often become too optimistic, and results in investors paying too much for the companies' shares. A good example is detailed in the Cisco / Intel story explained under Valuation Risk in chapter 3.

> "Market prices reflect investors' predictions about future growth, and the volatility is the natural consequence of the inevitable forecast errors."
> —Mordecai Kurz

The price one pays today drives future returns. The higher the price relative to intrinsic value, the higher the non-compensating risk the investor takes. History is full of investing lessons in which significantly overpaying for an asset results in lower-than-average future returns.

Appendix 4
Profitability Premium

Growth of gross profitability

The profitability premium is the excess return between stocks of companies with high profitability versus those with low profitability.

Profitability premium = High profitability company returns—low profitability returns

The profitability premium is the extra compensation for selecting companies with superior profitability. Profitability is measured as operating income before depreciation and amortization, minus interest expense divided by book value. Gross profitability is a powerful predictor of future growth, earnings, and free cash flows.

The profitability premium was explained in a 2012 paper by Professor Robert Novy-Marx, entitled "The Other Side of Value: The Gross Profitability Premium." Professor Novy-Marx, a world-renowned expert on empirical asset pricing, explored the relationships of different measures of current profitability to stock returns. His paper not only provided investors with new insights into the cross section of stock returns, it also helped explain Warren Buffett's superior performance—he invested in value companies with higher profitability metrics. Controlling for profitability dramatically increases the performance of value strategies, especially among the largest, most liquid stocks. Strategies based on gross profitability generate value-like average excess returns, even though they are growth strategies.

APPENDIX EXAMPLE 4.1: HIGH PROFITABILITY COMPANIES VERSUS LOW PROFITABILITY COMPANIES

Let us assume there are two companies that would like you to invest $50,000 in their common shares. With common shares, you are a fractional owner of the company. With ownership, you would participate in any growth of the company and any dividends that they could, or may choose to, pay shareholders. With ownership, if the business were to fail you could lose your total investment.

High Profitability Co is a medium-sized company and has been in business for twenty years. The company has achieved a solid growth of recurring gross profitability. The company is well entrenched within its industry.

Low Profitability Co is also a medium-sized company that has been in business for twenty years. The company has had its up and downs in growth over the years. Recently, a new product line has seen expected sales growth skyrocket, along with the company's share price. The growth of sales has not yet translated into persistent profitability.

What determines future returns is the price you pay and the growth of gross profitability. The key distinction is not the price to earnings or forecasted earnings, but the persistence of growing gross profitability. The profitability premium research helps sort the consistently profitable companies that execute on their business plans, from the inconsistent ones. In fact, research indicates the spread in the premium is a result of the disappointing profitability of the low profitability firms.

Other key findings to explain the premium:
- High profitability firms generate significantly higher returns than unprofitable firms, despite having high valuation ratios.
- High profitability firms tend to be growth firms—they expand comparatively quickly.
- Gross profitability has far more power in predicting the cross section of returns than earnings does.
- Small growth, low profitability companies are persistent underperformers.

The profitability premium is an overlay to broad market-based portfolios focused on value and small cap stocks. The profitability premium provides the value investment manager with a better filter to ensure they don't exclude highly profitable growth companies because they are using only standard valuation metrics.

Investing in highly profitable companies versus less profitable companies, assuming everything else is equal, should translate to higher expected returns. As noted in Appendix exhibit 4.1 the expectations are proven correct. Highly profitable companies experience share price returns that have historically been greater than that of less profitable companies.

APPENDIX EXHIBIT 4.1: HISTORICAL PROFITABILITY PREMIUMS

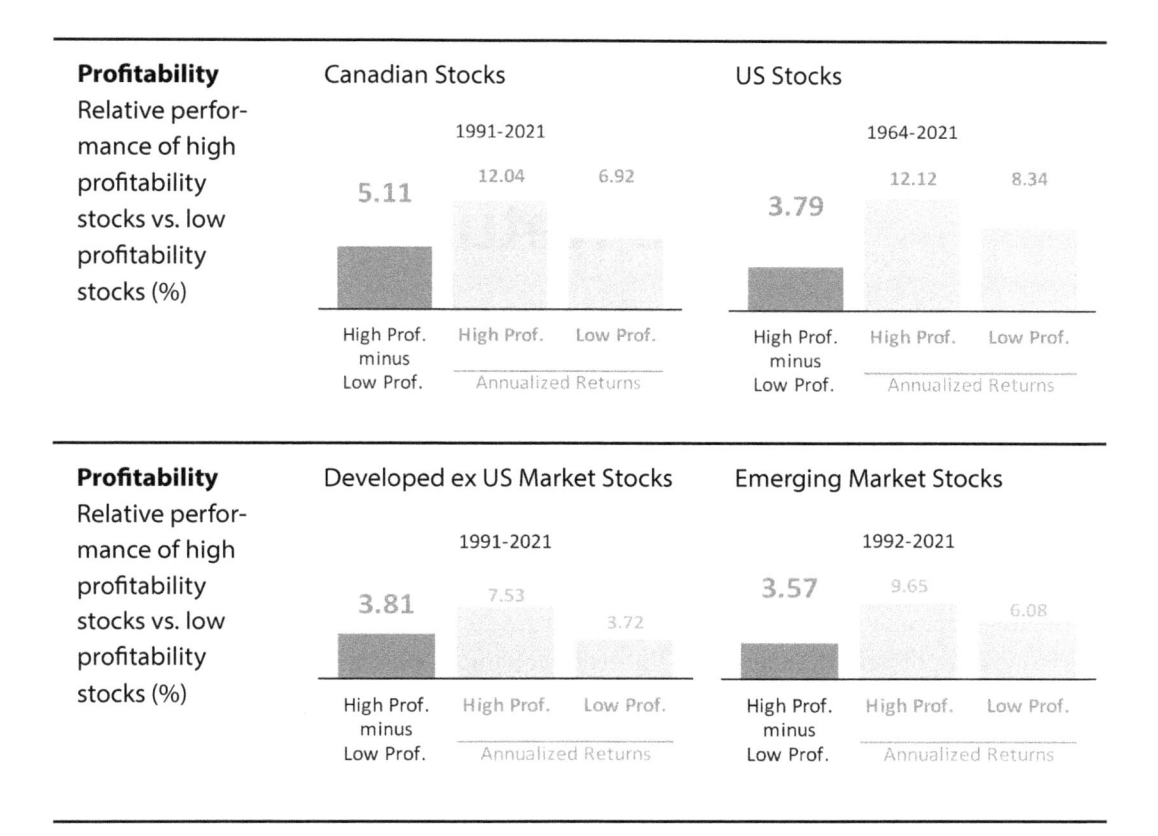

Profitability
Relative performance of high profitability stocks vs. low profitability stocks (%)

Canadian Stocks
1991-2021

High Prof. minus Low Prof.	High Prof.	Low Prof.
5.11	12.04	6.92

Annualized Returns

US Stocks
1964-2021

High Prof. minus Low Prof.	High Prof.	Low Prof.
3.79	12.12	8.34

Annualized Returns

Profitability
Relative performance of high profitability stocks vs. low profitability stocks (%)

Developed ex US Market Stocks
1991-2021

High Prof. minus Low Prof.	High Prof.	Low Prof.
3.81	7.53	3.72

Annualized Returns

Emerging Market Stocks
1992-2021

High Prof. minus Low Prof.	High Prof.	Low Prof.
3.57	9.65	6.08

Annualized Returns

Information provided by Dimensional Fund Advisors LP.

Information provided by Dimensional Fund Advisors LP.
Past performance is no guarantee of future results. Actual returns may be lower.
All returns are in USD, except Canadian stock returns, which are in CAD. MSCI indices are gross div. **Indices are not available for direct investment. Index returns are not representative of actual portfolios and do not reflect costs and fees associated with an actual investment.** For Canadian stocks, indices are used as follows. High Prof minus Low Prof: Fama/French Canada High Profitability Index minus the Fama/French Canada Low Profitability Index. For US stocks, indices are used as follows. High Prof minus Low Prof: Fama/French US High Profitability Index minus the Fama/French US Low Profitability Index. For developed ex US stocks, indices are used as follows. High Prof minus Low Prof: Fama/French International High Profitability Index minus the Fama/French International Low Profitability Index. For Emerging Markets stocks, indices are used as follows. High Prof minus Low Prof: Fama/French Emerging Markets High Profitability Index minus the Fama/French Emerging Markets Low Profitability Index. S&P and S&P/TSX data © 2022 S&P Dow Jones Indices LLC, a division of S&P Global. All rights reserved. MSCI data © MSCI 2022, all rights reserved.

Appendix 5

Randomness of Asset Class Returns

Markets don't die, they evolve

The fifty-plus markets around the world are home to companies competing for capital and human talent to push the envelope of human ingenuity. The companies compete to better serve consumer and societal demands while earning a profit to grow shareholder wealth. Investment opportunities exist across the ever-evolving global capital markets.

GLOBAL MARKET CAPITALIZATION:

- 60%   US
- 6%   Japan
- 4%   UK
- 4%   China
- 3%   France
- 3%   Switzerland
- 3%   Canada
- 2%   Germany
- 2%   Australia
- 1.5% India
- 1.5% South Korea
- 10%   Remainder of the world

GEOGRAPHIC MARKET CAPITALIZATION:

- 60%   US
- 24%   International
- 13%   Emerging markets
- 3%   Canada

Market capitalization, sometimes referred to as market cap, is the total value of a publicly traded company's outstanding common shares owned by stockholders. Market capitalization is equal to the market price per common share multiplied by the number of common shares outstanding. The US and developed markets market capitalization illustrate the benefits of democratic states with strong accounting, legal, and financial systems.

The past is not the future

APPENDIX EXHIBIT 5.1: RANDOMNESS OF RETURNS

The randomness of asset class returns is a good example of the lack of predictability in asset class performance from one year to the next. Global allocation and diversification across asset classes can help capture a broad range of returns and deliver more reliable outcomes over time.

Randomness of asset class returns

(Asset class description and explanation appear at the end of this Appendix.)

Asset Class:		1999	2000	2001	2002	2003	2004	2005	2006	2007	2008	2009	2010
Fixed Income	1	-1.8%	10.9%	7.9%	10.5%	6.8%	7.8%	5.7%	4.1%	3.3%	7.0%	7.5%	7.8%
Canada Large	2	31.7%	7.4%	-12.6%	-12.5%	26.7%	14.5%	24.1%	17.3%	9.8%	-33.0%	35.1%	17.6%
Canada Value	3	3.5%	28.3%	1.0%	-3.6%	27.8%	17.5%	21.4%	18.2%	2.1%	-32.5%	46.2%	16.4%
Canada Small	4	24.3%	2.0%	21.5%	-3.8%	36.3%	8.6%	10.7%	23.4%	3.9%	-46.9%	71.3%	38.2%
US Large	5	13.9%	-5.5%	-6.4%	-22.9%	5.5%	2.8%	2.3%	15.6%	-10.1%	-22.9%	9.3%	9.2%
US Value	6	0.4%	12.2%	1.6%	-16.0%	7.5%	8.4%	4.2%	22.1%	-15.6%	-21.9%	3.5%	10.3%
US Small	7	14.1%	0.8%	8.9%	-21.3%	20.7%	9.7%	1.9%	18.1%	-16.1%	-18.9%	9.9%	20.3%
International Large	8	29.4%	-16.3%	-18.2%	-16.4%	11.9%	9.7%	10.3%	25.6%	-3.6%	-29.9%	14.1%	1.5%
International Value	9	13.2%	-1.5%	-9.8%	-10.2%	18.8%	16.4%	11.3%	30.2%	-10.1%	-31.2%	18.0%	0.1%
International Small	10	13.1%	-3.6%	-6.6%	-8.3%	32.9%	21.7%	23.5%	19.4%	-13.3%	-34.8%	27.3%	16.1%
Emerging Markets	11	53.3%	-32.7%	4.3%	-7.2%	26.5%	17.8%	30.6%	31.8%	19.5%	-43.2%	58.0%	14.0%
Emerging Value	12	44.5%	-30.7%	11.2%	-0.5%	30.4%	22.9%	29.2%	32.4%	22.1%	-39.2%	58.6%	14.1%
Emerging Small	13	56.5%	-31.3%	9.3%	-2.4%	41.5%	23.3%	26.4%	38.6%	23.6%	-49.3%	80.8%	19.9%
Global REIT	14	-10.9%	28.4%	20.1%	6.8%	13.9%	24.1%	7.6%	38.5%	-24.3%	-32.7%	15.5%	17.1%

Randomness of asset class returns

(Asset class description and explanation appear at the end of this Appendix.)

Asset Class:		2011	2012	2013	2014	2015	2016	2017	2018	2019	2020	2021	2022
Fixed Income	1	10.9%	4.6%	-0.6%	9.2%	4.9%	1.6%	1.0%	1.9%	5.8%	10.1%	-2.7%	-10.3%
Canada Large	2	-8.7%	7.2%	13.0%	10.6%	-8.3%	21.1%	9.1%	-8.9%	22.9%	5.6%	25.1%	-5.8%
Canada Value	3	-5.2%	11.7%	16.0%	3.1%	-12.4%	32.4%	9.5%	-10.2%	21.8%	-7.5%	35.9%	1.9%
Canada Small	4	-12.7%	0.5%	8.4%	1.1%	-13.9%	27.8%	6.3%	-12.7%	24.8%	16.1%	22.8%	-5.6%
US Large	5	4.3%	13.0%	41.6%	24.3%	20.8%	8.7%	14.0%	3.8%	25.1%	16.1%	28.0%	-12.3%
US Value	6	2.0%	14.5%	42.0%	23.3%	14.2%	14.9%	5.9%	-0.7%	20.1%	0.9%	24.7%	-1.5%
US Small	7	-2.1%	13.4%	48.5%	14.7%	13.8%	17.7%	7.3%	-3.4%	19.4%	17.6%	14.2%	-14.8%
International Large	8	-9.4%	14.8%	31.6%	3.8%	17.2%	-1.4%	16.6%	-5.1%	16.2%	5.4%	12.2%	-6.2%
International Value	9	-10.5%	15.8%	33.3%	4.0%	14.5%	2.7%	15.4%	-7.4%	12.0%	-3.4%	11.1%	0.1%
International Small	10	-13.8%	17.3%	38.8%	4.3%	30.9%	-0.5%	24.9%	-10.5%	19.4%	10.5%	9.9%	-15.5%
Emerging Markets	11	-17.5%	16.0%	5.0%	7.8%	3.0%	7.0%	28.5%	-7.4%	12.3%	16.5%	-0.5%	-13.8%
Emerging Value	12	-16.9%	14.1%	2.5%	6.1%	-1.0%	11.3%	21.4%	-3.4%	6.9%	4.6%	5.4%	-8.9%
Emerging Small	13	-22.5%	22.2%	8.7%	11.0%	10.3%	9.8%	26.7%	-9.6%	9.5%	12.3%	15.3%	-13.2%
Global REIT	14	3.9%	20.6%	10.0%	34.3%	19.8%	3.8%	1.7%	3.4%	18.4%	-9.9%	31.8%	-18.2%

7 STEPS TO A BETTER PORTFOLIO | 163

ASSET CLASS DESCRIPTIONS:

	Asset class:	Benchmark:
1)	Bonds	FTSE Canadian Mid-Term Bond Index
2)	Canada Large	S&P/TSX Composite Index
3)	Canada Value	MSCI Canada IMI Value Index (gross div., CAD)
4)	Canada Small	MSCI Canada Small Cap Index (gross div.)
5)	US Large	S&P 500 Index
6)	US Value	Russell 3000 Value Index
7)	US Small	Russell 2000 Index
8)	International Large	MSCI EAFE Large Cap Index (gross div.)
9)	International Value	MSCI EAFE IMI Value Index (gross div.)
10)	International Small	MSCI EAFE Small Cap Index (gross div.)
11)	Emerging Markets	MSCI Emerging Markets IMI Index (gross div.)
12)	Emerging Markets	MSCI Emerging Markets IMI Value Index (gross div.)
13)	Emerging Markets	MSCI Emerging Markets IMI Small Cap Index (gross div.)
14)	Global Real Estate	S&P Global REIT Index (gross div.)

All returns reported in Canadian dollars CAD

Gross dividend (gross div) defined:
A gross dividend equals the dividends paid out, without subtracting taxes, fees, or other costs.

Information provided by Dimensional Fund Advisors LP.

In Canadian dollars. Charts are for illustrative purposes only. Canadian Fixed Income is FTSE Canada Mid-Term Bond Index. Canadian Large Cap is the S&P/TSX Composite Index. Canadian Value is the MSCI Canada IMI Value Index (gross div.). Canadian Small Cap is the MSCI Canada Small Cap Index (gross div.). US Large Cap is the S&P 500 Index. US Value is Russell 3000 Value Index. US Small Cap is Russell 2000 Index. US Real Estate is the Dow Jones US Select REIT Index. International Large Cap is the MSCI EAFE Large Cap Index (gross div.), and International Value is the MSCI EAFE IMI Value Index (gross div.). International Small Cap is MSCI EAFE Small Cap Index (gross div.). FTSE fixed income indices © 2020 FTSE Fixed Income LLC. All rights reserved. MSCI data © MSCI 2020, all rights reserved. S&P, S&P/TSX and Dow Jones data © 2020 S&P Dow Jones Indices LLC, a division of S&P Global. All rights reserved. Frank Russell Company is the source and owner of the trademarks, service marks, and copyrights related to the Russell Indexes. **Indices are not available for direct investment. Index performance does not reflect the expenses associated with the management of an actual portfolio. Past performance is not a guarantee of future results. Actual returns may be lower.**

Structure / Structure / Structure

Allocate across global capital markets
Diversify broadly within markets
Focus on higher expected returns
Utilize financial science
Manage strategy risk
Manage investment choice risk
Manage costs and taxes

A rules-based, systematic portfolio process and structure

Institutional pension style portfolio management

7stepstoabetterportfolio.com

Something is Happening!

New information and opinions may agree or disagree with our investment feelings. Information and opinions can push and pull us in many directions. It is a psychological battle between what makes us feel fearful, hopeful, and comfortable.

A rules-based systematic process and structure can act as a decision-making framework. It can guide you to better manage the variables you can control to better manage the variables you can't.

Factors to consider:
- Long-term – rather than short term
- Rules based – rather than disorganized and haphazard
- Proactive policy driven approach – rather than forecast driven
- Evidence-based research – rather than noisy unsubstantiated information
- Trust in the process – rather than excessive worry and anxiousness
- Manage bias – rather than let bias impact decision making
- Task oriented – rather than procrastination
- Probable versus possible
- Focus on what matters

Change the way you think about investing! Improve your odds of a successful outcome by utilizing the *7 Steps*:

1) Allocate across global capital markets
2) Diversify broadly within markets
3) Focus on higher expected returns
4) Utilize financial science
5) Manage strategy risk
6) Manage investment choice risk
7) Manage costs and taxes

Portfolio investing is math and emotion. Math is how we should build and manage a portfolio. Emotion is why we don't. Math will improve the odds of a successful outcome. Emotion will create more randomness and excitement.

Ingram Content Group UK Ltd.
Milton Keynes UK
UKHW032349050723
424591UK00008B/379